LACE
KNITTING

LACE KNITTING

Helen James

THE CROWOOD PRESS

First published in 2019 by
The Crowood Press Ltd
Ramsbury, Marlborough
Wiltshire SN8 2HR

www.crowood.com

British Library Cataloguing-in-Publication Data
A catalogue record for this book is available from the British Library.

ISBN 978 1 78500 571 8

Typeset by Peggy & Co. Design Inc.
Printed and bound in India by Parksons Graphics

CONTENTS

Preface

I have been a knitter for most of my life, and like many people of my generation, was fortunate enough to have been taught the basics as a child at school, in a post war era that still considered the teaching of such skills as a necessary part of every child's education. Like many children, I was encouraged to practise my embryonic knitting skills under the watchful eyes of the female members of my family, all of whom were proficient knitters themselves. My earliest creation – at the age of six years old – was a pair of pale-yellow fluffy bed socks with an eyelet pattern in the cuff. The mistakes were many but I loved those socks because they were to my mind lacy and therefore pretty.

Lace, it seems, has always held a fascination. Attempts to teach me how to make tatted lace when I was about seven years old were not very successful, ending in a tangled mess. Nevertheless, despite this early frustration I continued to love all things lacy. For many years I had no idea that the incredibly fine, airy and romantic lace that I was so attracted to could actually be knitted. However, the realization came as something of a revelation in adulthood when quite by chance I found an old book containing a limited number of written down patterns, for motifs described as Shetland lace. I was intrigued that this book seemed to suggest that a reasonably competent knitter could create this beautiful fabric that I had loved since childhood. I was not however convinced, as to my mind the pattern seemed very complicated, but I decided that I would try to knit the pattern anyway and see what happened. I chose to

The first lace swatch I ever knitted. Pale-yellow lace-weight cashmere and extremely small needles produced a dense but very soft fabric.

try a small swatch of Fern lace with small needles, using some fine cashmere yarn. The smallness of the needles resulted in a denser fabric than I had anticipated but I loved it nevertheless and still have it. I soon learnt that larger needles and fine yarn make lighter, airier lace. I was from that point on completely captivated and have continued to explore and experiment with lace ever since.

More recently along my knitting journey I obtained the City and Guilds Certificate in Hand Knit and Design, which taught me much, including how much more there always is to learn.

List of abbreviations and symbols

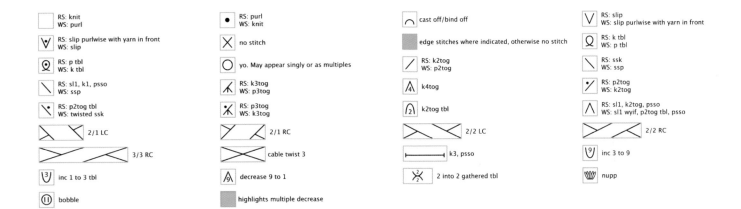

Key to symbols used in this book.

k: knit

p: purl

st(s): stitch(es)

RS: right-side

WS: wrong-side

DK: double knit

dpn: double pointed needle

M1: make 1

M1l: make 1 left

M1r: make 1 right

yo: yarn over

ssk: slip, slip, knit

skp: slip, knit, pass slip stitch over

k2tog: knit 2 stitches together

k3tog: knit 3 stitches together

p2tog: purl 2 stitches together

p3tog: purl 3 stitches together

k tbl: knit through back of loop

psso: pass slip stitch over

sl1, k2tog, psso: slip 1, knit 2 together, pass slip stitch over

wyif: with yarn in front

INTRODUCTION

The aim of this book is to share my passion and fascination with lace knitting and to show that, providing you have acquired the essential basic skills of knitting, creating lace is something that can be achieved – no matter how daunted you may feel. Much of it looks more complicated than it actually is and although it does require some concentration, it should be well within the grasp of the average knitter. You, however, would be well advised against embarking upon your first lace project when you are very tired or sitting in front of the TV as your ability to count and keep track of your stitches will be more impaired than you might imagine. Similarly, it would not be a good idea to jump straight in by knitting a complex lace shawl. Practise motifs separately to begin with, get the feel of knitted lace and then look at more complex designs as your skill and understanding develop.

A good place to begin might be to look at my suggestion later in the book for knitting the motifs in a heavier weight yarn in a variety of colours on large needles, and then crocheting the varying sized swatches together in a contrasting yarn to make a sampler blanket.

Whilst this is not a book of patterns, there are some in the form of projects for you to try out and vary as you wish. I hope to inspire those of you who may be less familiar with this area of knitting to take that first step and start to explore this fascinating genre, to develop your skills, and to encourage beginners and more confident knitters alike to explore the medium of lace knitting, not solely by the following of patterns created by others but through a study of lace motifs, techniques and use of inspirational materials to create your own unique pieces. I invite you to look at ways of taking something seen as traditional, explore how it can be used in a more contemporary manner and then use it to both enhance and inspire your own projects.

By following patterns created by others you can learn a great deal about the technical creation of lace. You can begin to understand how motifs can work together, learn how to read your lace knitting, practise manipulating yarns thinner than you might normally use, and marvel at the skill and ingenuity of the lace knitters of past centuries who created these beautiful patterns without any kind of written recording or charts, and without the very great advantage of electric light.

Harebell lace wedding wrap, knitted in a lace weight, extra fine Merino yarn. This wrap has a lovely drape and is light and floaty, feeling truly luxurious.

If you are a curious and interested knitter, you will be aware that there is more to lace knitting, and indeed all aspects of knitting than purely repeating a pattern, notwithstanding the immense satisfaction that can be gained by the completion of a complex design. By stepping out from the safety of the written pattern you truly gain an opportunity to explore lace knitting from a different perspective. Undoubtedly on occasions things will not turn out as you expect, you will make mistakes or just not like the result, but it does not matter. The beauty of exploring any aspect of knitting is that it is easy to unravel the piece and start again, hopefully wiser than before. It is also entirely possible that a mistake may open a door to new ideas or variations on an existing idea or motif and lead to an outcome that is unexpected and both beautiful and unique.

How to use this book

The next few paragraphs provide important information as to the way in which this book should be used. Skip the introduction and background reading by all means, but please do read the next few paragraphs so that you do not immediately turn to the pattern section and wonder why some of the patterns are less detailed than you might have expected.

Over the coming pages this book will explain the basic techniques of lace knitting, and provide you with the skills to interpret patterns and charts with confidence.

There are some projects in this book; however, some are deliberately less detailed than others, providing a template for you to use as a starting point, with suggestions as to how you might progress rather than using detailed instructions on how to complete the item.

Other patterns are more complete but provide nudges to look at different options for their completion, for example, the wedding wrap design shown here, and featured in Chapters 7 and 9. All the patterns are adaptable and you are encouraged to explore different options rather than just replicating my particular approach, although of course you are free to do this as well if you wish.

In order to get the best from this book you should have the following basic skills: be able to knit and purl, undertake basic increases, yarn overs and decreases, and follow a written pattern. Information is provided about more unusual types of increases and decreases, along with specific types of casting on and off that work well with lace.

If you are new to lace knitting, there are suggestions as to which motifs you might like to try initially so that you can build on your skills and work up to some of the more complex patterns. This will also provide you with the opportunity to become accustomed to the way in which the yarn-over increases and the paired decreases work. You can then move on to motifs where the increase and decrease are separated by one or more stitches and eventually even one or more rows, as for the delayed decrease. The projects at the end of the book provide very easy lace motifs for new lace knitters, as well as complex patterns for those with some lace knitting experience.

The following chapters will provide information about the tools that you will need and yarns and how they perform when knitted as lace; detailed explanations for using charts; understanding abbreviations; finishing techniques including blocking, and the development of your own designs. There is a Stitchionary containing lace motifs, insertions and edgings, with both charts and written instructions. There are a vast number of lace motifs and stitches and it is not the aim of this book to provide a definitive overview of the thousands of patterns and variations that are available, but rather to suggest sufficient stitch patterns to get you started and sign posts to aid further exploration of further patterns and traditions of lace knitting.

Lace sampler from the Knitting and Crochet Guild collection. A good place to visit
if you are interested in further research.

CHAPTER 1

A BRIEF HISTORY OF LACE KNITTING

For many, it is the fine, white, wedding ring shawls of great complexity and beauty that spring to mind when first thinking about lace knitting.

It is the areas of Shetland, Estonia and Orenburg that provide the current main interest in knitted lace today, each with its own unique tradition and history of producing these shawls.

This interest in fine knitted lace, much loved and highly sought after by the Victorians across Europe, has enjoyed something of a revival in recent times and there are many skilled knitters who both enjoy recreating the old patterns and producing shawls and wraps of considerable beauty as well as producing new designs, all of which is contributing to the continued development and indeed survival of this fascinating art. But where did it come from?

It is widely believed that knitting originated in the Middle East and that it emanated from there through Spain during the Crusades in the twelfth and thirteenth centuries, and it is thought to have arrived in England in the mid thirteenth century.

Lace knitting, like knitting in general, has a fascinating history. It is not really known where it originated, but the earliest known example of lace in knitting is thought to be a pair of silk knitted hose featuring a diagonal Faggot pattern dated to the mid 1500s and which is housed at the Dresden Museum. Eleanora di Toledo, the Grand Duchess of Tuscany, who died in 1562, was found to have been buried in a pair of silk lace stockings. Elizabeth I of England is thought to be

An example of fine Shetland Lace from the collection at the Unst Heritage Centre, Haroldswick.

This is an example of Estonian lace knitting, the Maikel shawl from a pattern by Nancy Bush.

A gate to a beach warning of mermaids, who are associated in folklore with the origins of lace.

the first British monarch to wear silk stockings. It is said that in 1560 a Mrs Montague, who was a lady in waiting to Elizabeth, presented the Queen with a gift of knitted silk stockings with a diamond lace motif. The story maintains that the Queen was so taken with these stockings that she had Mrs Montague make her more. Indeed, there is a pair of lacy knit stockings in this design, said to be of approximately the right age, on display at Hatfield House, the childhood home of the Queen. Whilst this does suggest that lace knitting was a recognized skill in the mid 1500s, it is simply not known if there is any truth to this particular story. It is suggested in the literature that this pattern may have originated in France, but nobody actually knows.

The earliest inklings of lace associated with the Shetland Isles were found with the remains of the 'Gunnister Man', discovered in a peat bog near Gunnister, Shetland, in 1951. The remains were subsequently dated to 1680–90, so somewhat later than the earlier examples of lace from Dresden, Italy and Queen Bess's stockings. Alongside the preserved knitted garments

found with the body was a fragment of knitting of a lace diamond motif created from yarn-over increases and decreases. Debate continues as to whether or not Gunnister Man was a local or a visiting sailor, due to the Dutch and Swedish coins that were found with him, but whatever his origins, this small fragment of knitted lace suggests that lace knitting might have been known and possibly practised in Shetland earlier than the current evidential base is able to demonstrate.

Because of the lack of evidence or a clearly established timeline for the development of knitted lace, there is a certain mystique about its origins. This has led to legends and folklore as to how it began in different parts of the world. Perhaps my favourite is the story from Shetland that a mermaid wove together the foam from the waves to make a garment so that she could be appropriately clad whilst on dry land visiting the fisherman that she loved. It is told that the islanders were so taken with this garment that they set about trying to copy it, thus creating the lovely lace with which the islands are associated.

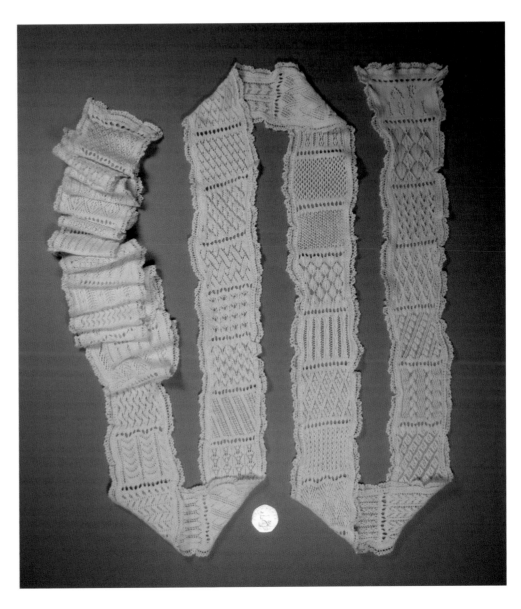

Example of a sampler showing the skill of the knitters. This can be seen in the collection of the Knitting and Crochet Guild.

In the past, the traditions of knitting were handed down from generation to generation, by word of mouth, with children learning the knitted patterns from their parents, grandparents and other family members. Lace knitting traditions were shared in the same way, and whilst it may seem amazing to us, patterns, including the most complex, were committed to memory, and were knitted and shared without ever being recorded. Despite the lack of written patterns, it seems likely that knowledge of the patterns travelled from place to place, which would in part explain the similarity of motifs in lace knitting from various parts of the world. There is little doubt that historically there was far more travel, particularly overseas, than might hitherto have been imagined, with well-established

routes between Northern Europe, the Shetland Islands and Southern Europe, dating back to the days of the Vikings. This would have allowed the knowledge of designs, techniques and motifs to move with sailors and travellers passing through, and to then be copied and further developed or adapted by knitters in their own countries.

Any hope that the names of the lace patterns might shed some light as to their origins rapidly vanishes after any initial research. Many of the patterns are named for the everyday things that people saw around them, for example, leaves, paws, flowers, insects and birds to name but a few. However, it quickly becomes apparent that the names of lace patterns are frequently confusing, with the same names being used to describe different motifs, and the same motifs cropping up in different lace traditions with different names. For example, the Estonian Peacock Tail motif is the same as the Shetland Horseshoe lace motif, but which came first? Nobody knows.

As lace knitting became more popular, it became a leisure pastime of wealthy Victorian women, as well as continuing to be an income-generating pastime in places such as Shetland, Orenburg and Estonia. Victorian ladies created samplers of their patterns as an *aide-memoire* and to show off their skills. These are often extremely intricate, and provide a fascinating insight into the skill of these knitters in times past. Many of these have survived and can be found housed in museums around the world.

The written published pattern is a relatively recent development in the world of knitting, only becoming established in the Victorian era when printed pamphlets containing 'receipts' for knitted goods increasingly became available.

Early written patterns provide a fascinating glimpse into the development of pattern writing, but can be more or less indecipherable to today's knitter, with authors having their own shorthand and symbols for the instructions which need to be patiently decoded by today's knitter, a challenging exercise and not for the faint-hearted! Not all patterns were accurate, and some were downright impossible, suggesting a lack of testing in some cases before publication!

The written pattern in a form that is more widely recognized today became increasingly common in the early part of the twentieth century. Patterns for knitted items during both world wars were readily available with much encouragement from the government of the day to knit for the war effort. After the Second World War, knitting patterns became increasingly commonplace and were widely published in women's magazines, and became readily available in any outlet that also sold yarn. Whilst it is possible to find patterns from the post war era for lace, much of what was available was less intricate than the fine lace knitting of the past and often took the form of lacy baby blankets, evening stoles or cardigans. In recent years, however, with the rise of the internet and the increased interest in fine lace knitting, written and charted patterns for extremely intricate lace shawls are now widely available. The majority of books of stitches will include some lace motifs, and specialist books relating to specific lace traditions are now available.

In conclusion, whilst it is impossible to say where or how the knitting of lace evolved, given that there are such distinct similarities in many aspects of design across the different lace traditions both from northern and southern Europe, it would be difficult to believe that they each developed in isolation from one another.

The extent to which overseas trade and travel was happening in earlier centuries is not always recognized but the fact that Shetland and Orenburg, for example, were based in strategically important areas in terms of trade routes, together with Shetland's fishing industry which also attracted travellers, must surely have had some bearing on the early development of lace knitting. Similarly, travel to and from England to all parts of Europe and beyond was well established by the nineteenth century and equally opened another route for ideas, techniques and designs to travel. Consequently, it is very difficult to believe that each knitted lace tradition emerged, fully formed in the mid nineteenth century. Due to the lack of physical evidence, however, it is quite possible that we will never really know for sure where lace knitting first emerged, nor be able to track its development over the centuries.

The whole picture is further complicated by the ease with which patterns started to be published and widely shared after the Second World War and the now almost instant availability across the globe of knitting patterns from around the world by virtue of the internet. This has resulted in so many crossovers of designs from many different places that it is now very difficult indeed to really attribute specific patterns as having originated in a particular place. This adds a continuing degree of mystery to the knitting of lace. For those who are interested in pursuing this aspect of knitting history, there are ample opportunities for further research and study and I have included some sources for further reading and exploration in the bibliography at the end of this book.

Shetland Lace

Prior to 1832, when Shetland lace knitting was first observed, there is a record of Shetlanders producing socks and woollen stockings dating back to at least the early 1600s, clearly suggesting that they were skilled knitters and spinners. By the 1800s, the islanders had established a reputation for the production of fine knitted stockings, although still continued to produce coarse knitted stockings, socks and mitts. These were traded with foreign sailors, many from Holland and Germany.

Amongst the alternative theories as to how the Shetlanders discovered lace knitting are suggestions that it came from the mainland in the 1830s, or that lace was brought from Brussels and shown to a family of knitters on the island of Unst which inspired them to develop lace knitting. If this is the case, then this skill was one that was learned and shared very quickly amongst the islanders as it is recorded that the export of fine

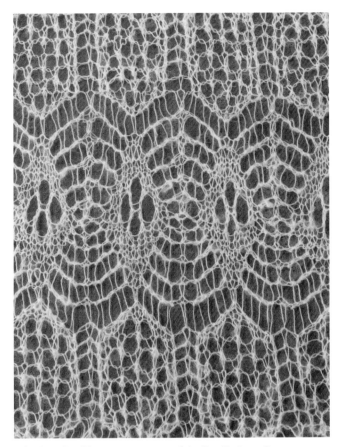

A fine lace shawl from Unst, courtesy of the Unst Heritage Centre.

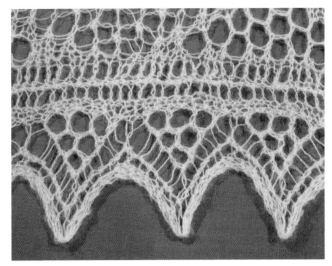

This edging from a fine lace shawl from the collection held by the Unst Heritage Centre shows how effective the use of yarn over increases and knit 2 together decreases can be.

Shetland sheep enjoying the rain.

lace knit shawls from the Shetlands was well established by the mid to late 1840s.

Whilst nobody knows where Shetland lace originated, there must be a possibility, given the level of complexity of design and expertise of the knitters, that this skill had been practised for some time before it was spotted in the 1830s. We do not, however, have any evidence to support this theory, largely because of a lack of examples of surviving knitted lace from this area pre-dating the 1830s other than the tantalizing glimpse of knitted lace with the remains of the Gunnister Man.

It is also evident that the motifs found in Shetland lace knitting are markedly similar to those seen in many other parts of the world. There are a large number of motifs that are today described as Shetland in origin. Mary Thomas recorded that she had been told by a family of well-known Shetland lace knitters that there were only ten motifs that were truly Shetland in origin and she lists these as: Ears o' Grain, Cat's Paw, Print o' the Wave, Birds Eye, Fern, Fir Cone, Spout Shell, Old Shale, Acre

and Horseshoe (Richard Rutt, *A History of Hand Knitting*). Again it is simply not possible to know. Any examination of some of the more common motifs such as Cat's Paw and Horseshoe lace will demonstrate the remarkable similarity across various lace traditions. For those interested, the paper by Elizabeth Lovick, 'Knitting Beyond the Hebrides, The Same but Different' provides an intriguing examination of some of these motifs.

From the mid 1830s, the popularity of knitted Shetland lace increased dramatically, and it was in great demand by fashionable Victorian ladies and favoured by the Queen. It soon became the primary occupation of women on the islands who produced lace

This is an example of an Orenburg shawl bought in St Petersburg, Russia. As you can see, it shows some of the traditional motifs associated with Orenburg lace.

shawls in great quantity. It is, however, a sad fact that the lace knitters often earned very little from their skills and endeavours and, in some cases, were paid in kind rather than in cash.

Shetland lace is largely based on garter stitch. Purl stitches slowed the lace knitters down and as they were knitting for money, they needed to be able to knit as efficiently as possible, and thus garter stitch was preferred. Shetland lace uses yarn-over increases paired with knit 2 together and knit 3 together decreases to create an array of beautiful patterns.

In order to produce lace of the quality found in Shetland, you need the right kind of wool. The success of the knitted lace from Shetland is in no small measure contingent upon the suitability of the yarn from the sheep native to those islands.

The sheep of the Shetland Islands are a particular breed, producing soft strong wool, which when spun creates a yarn with excellent stitch definition. The fineness of the yarn and the skill of the spinners is frequently commented upon in the historical commentaries of the 1800s, with the quality of the yarn spun on the Island of Unst being noted as being particularly fine.

The reputation of the fineness of the lace produced on Unst during the 1800s and 1900s has remained. Examples of Unst lace can be seen at the Unst Heritage Centre and the Lerwick Textile Museum, both of which also house an impressive collection of fine lace Shetland shawls.

In the 1840s, as written patterns, or 'receipts', began to appear with patterns and designs within them, they regularly included patterns described as Shetland, alongside a variety of lace patterns attributed variously as French, Irish or Spanish, or simply as a pretty open pattern for a shawl. Collections of these patterns can still be found contained in the old pattern books of the late 1800s and early 1900s by Weldon, Lambert and Gaugain, amongst others.

Over the twentieth century, as travel became ever more accessible and patterns travelled to other parts of the world, their names were often changed, thus adding to the confusion as to the place from which a pattern might have originated. Nowadays with so much cross-fertilization of ideas and patterns, it is very difficult to really know where any particular motif described as Shetland lace might have originated, and never more so than with the advent of the internet which provides a huge resource of patterns from across the globe at the press of a button.

Orenburg Lace

Orenburg is a city situated in south-eastern Russia, close to the border of both Asia and Europe, and borders Kazakhstan.

An Orenburg shawl showing the edges and border motifs.

Despite the apparent remoteness of its situation, Orenburg was a central point on the trade routes between Russia, Europe and Asia. This is an interesting parallel with the Shetland Islands, another remote location with the benefit of being situated on the European trade routes. Orenburg knitted lace appears to have a history dating back to the mid 1700s, thus predating any knowledge of a knitted lace tradition in Shetland by at least a hundred years. That does not mean it was not happening, just that we have no evidence that it was.

As with other knitted lace traditions, there are no real facts as to where or how this tradition was established, although there are of course tales and folklore associated with its origins.

By the mid eighteenth century, such was the demand for the warm knitted shawls of Orenburg, that it was the pre-eminent occupation of women and girls in the Orenburg area of Russia and, like Shetland Lace, it rapidly gained in popularity across Europe. It should also be said that like the women of Shetland, the Orenburg knitters often gained very little from their efforts in creating breathtakingly beautiful lace as the production of knitted lace was managed by middlemen who appear to have exploited the knitters for their own considerable profit.

Orenburg Lace is typified by both large, warm, square shawls and by extremely beautiful gossamer shawls with complex designs derived from combining the basic stitch patterns of this tradition in a huge variety of ways. Traditionally the only three stitches in Orenburg Lace are knit 2 together, sometimes knit 3 together, yarn over and knit. There is no purl stitch as this was not used as is the case in the Shetland tradition. This makes the design and construction of the lace a very skilled undertaking, by using the simple motifs in a myriad of different arrangements to create the beautiful designs associated with this tradition. The motifs that these complex designs are based upon are named for the everyday things that people saw around them, for example, Peas, Fish Eyes, Mouse Paws and Strawberries. It is only very recently that these designs have been turned into charts for others to use. Traditionally the lace knitters of Orenburg learnt to knit the patterns whilst still very young and committed them to memory.

The Orenburg shawl derives its warmth and fineness from the particular yarn from which it is made. The yarn is traditionally made from a specific breed of goat that is peculiar to this area of Orenburg in Eastern Russia. The down is combed from the animal. An average of two pounds of down can be taken from an adult goat. The down is then cleaned and spun ready for knitting.

The fibre derived from Orenburg goats is said to be the finest in the world and to be finer and warmer than Cashmere. It is exceptionally soft and warm and is routinely plied to the fineness of commercial silk, providing the gossamer threads for the construction of the finest shawls. In the 1800s, much of the down from these goats was exported to Europe. It was, however, expensive so it was hoped that the goats themselves could be bred in Europe, thus making the acquisition of this sought after fibre more cost effective and generally available. The subsequent attempts to produce the down outside of the Orenburg area ultimately met with failure, as it seems that the exceptional qualities of the fibre so valued by the lace knitter is only produced by the goats in response to the extreme harshness of the Eastern Russian climate and, after a year or two of living in warmer climes, their coats changed and the soft downy undercoat became coarser and weaker and lost its insulating properties, with the result that it was no longer suitable for the knitting of these shawls. For those interested in experimenting with this yarn, it can be obtained online from the Orenburg area of Russia.

Estonian Lace

Estonian Lace is now a widely recognized lace tradition of Europe, typified by beautiful, cobwebby white wool shawls. Historically the centre of this development was the Estonian seaside resort town of Haapsalu, an extremely pretty town situated on the west coast of Estonia. What put it on the map was the establishment in 1852 of a mud bath spa in the town. This drew in wealthy visitors from Russia who travelled to enjoy the baths. The flow of wealthy tourists also included members of the Russian royal family whose patronage made the resort even more fashionable. This provided ample opportunity for the women of Haapsalu to find a vibrant market for their exquisite knitted shawls, which became increasingly popular as a consequence. The thriving industry provided funds to help the families survive the harsh winters, during which they employed their time knitting the next batch of shawls ready for the following season's influx of visitors. The production of these shawls declined for entirely understandable reasons during the First World War, following which Estonia became an independent republic in 1918. Subsequently production was re-established and the fame of the white shawls of Haapsalu again began to spread and soon they were being traded across the world.

Today the production of Haapsalu shawls continues and there is now widespread interest in learning the techniques associated with the creation of this beautiful lace tradition.

Many of the motifs seen in Estonian Lace bear a marked resemblance to motifs from other knitted lace traditions and there are striking similarities to some of the Shetland patterns.

Estonian Lace uses a more complex construction than either the Shetland or Orenburg Lace tradition. It is generally knitted on a stocking stitch ground, and twisted stitches, mass increases and decreases and purl stitch can all be found in this lace tradition. Although Estonian Lace has many patterns and variations, it is perhaps most commonly associated with a particular type of bobble known as a 'nupp' (rhymes with soup!), which provides a texture to the lace designs. Perhaps the best-known motif is that of the Lily of the Valley, a beautiful and versatile motif that can be created with or without nupps, and of which there are many versions. Leaf motifs are also very popular within the Estonian tradition, as are twigs, flowers, grain and insects.

There are variations across the traditions in some aspects of traditional shawl construction and whilst with Shetland shawls the edges are either worked in one piece or knitted on, and Orenburg shawls are worked in one piece, in the Estonian tradition the edges are knitted separately and then sewn on.

There are, however, many more similarities seen in the traditional patterns of Estonian Lace with lace attributed to not only the Shetland and Orenburg tradition but with lace that is seen more generally across Europe. Compare the Estonian Head of Grain pattern, frequently found in Estonian Stitch Dictionaries, with the Shetland Fern Lace, for example, or the Twig pattern with two lines from Estonia with the Print of the Wave pattern from Shetland or the leaf patterns from Estonia with the many variations of this motif from around the world.

Estonian Peacock Tail wrap from a pattern by Nancy Bush. Note the similarity with Horseshoe lace.

CHAPTER 2

GETTING STARTED

So, before we start we need to establish what is knitted lace. Knitted lace is a fabric created by the knitter using a combination of yarn-over increases paired with decreases. This creates a fabric of patterned holes. The variations of design using this basic construction method are enormous.

It is the yarn-over increases that make the holes in lace. Larger holes can easily be created by increasing the times that the yarn is wrapped around the needle.

In Estonian Lace you will find that a combination of yarn-overs and knitting into the same stitch multiple times are used to create either a mass increase, such as in Flower stitch, or nupps. Nevertheless, the basic principle of yarn over increases paired with decreases remains.

Lace knitting and knitted lace are both frequently used terms for describing this craft, and are more often these days used interchangeably as they are in this book. There is, however, traditionally a difference of meaning attributed to each of these terms as follows: lace knitting is a lace pattern with plain knit or purl stitches on the alternate rows, thus only patterning on one side; knitted lace is knitted with patterning on every row which tends to create lace with more holes and thus produces an airier, more lacy fabric.

In order to successfully knit lace, you will require some tools, and a key to understand both the abbreviations used in the written patterns and the symbols used in the charts. In addition, you will find it helpful to acquire needles with fine, sharp points to assist in the knitting of fine yarn and the manipulation of the decreases.

This chapter will provide information about yarn with some indication of the performance of various yarns in relation to lace knitting. There is also a section specifically looking at the use of charts with instructions on how to read these.

Tools

Knitting Needles of Various Sizes

Circular needles, either fixed or with interchangeable tips, are very useful for large projects, and for knitting in the round, for example, for the Hap throw. Nowadays there is often a preference for circular needles although traditionally lace has been knitted on straight or double pointed needles. One advantage of circulars is that they spread the weight of larger projects more evenly, and when travelling, you are much less likely to lose a needle down the side of a train seat!

For some, straight single needles will always be the option of choice, and if this is you then it is helpful to have a variety of different lengths to cope with different sizes of projects. Double

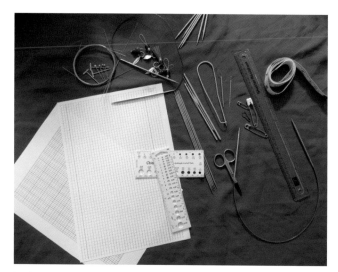
Tools you will need to knit lace.

pointed needles (dpns) are also an important part of a lace knitter's tool kit and are used traditionally by the Shetland lace knitters in combination with a knitting sheath. Demonstrations of this method of knitting can be found on YouTube. Ultimately it really does not matter what kind of needle you use; there are no right or wrong needles, and what you choose is very much a question of personal preference. It is, however, important for the knitting of lace that needles have sharp points. Blunt points make it very difficult to knit the fine lace yarn and manipulate the decrease stitches. Needles designed specifically for lace knitting are widely available and if using circulars, it is important to ensure that the join between the needle and the wire is as seamless as possible as any gap, even the smallest, will inevitably snag your fine yarn, which is a real nuisance and occasionally disastrous. This is true of both fixed and interchangeable circular needles. Needles are available in an assortment of colours, but it is worth remembering that having a needle that contrasts with the colour of your yarn will make knitting your lace much easier. There is nothing worse than trying to see what you are doing whilst knitting a fine dark yarn on a black or dark wood needle, for example.

A Needle Gauge

This is essential, you should have at least one. I have several as they have a bad habit of vanishing when most needed. These are necessary as some circular needles and double pointed needles lose the written indication of size quite quickly, whilst circulars are extremely small and difficult to read, so a needle gauge allows a quick and convenient way to check the size of your needles. The additional advantage of a needle gauge is

that most have needle sizes in Imperial and US gauges as well as millimetres, which allows you to translate old needle sizes into current millimetre sizes or US gauges with ease.

Crochet Hooks of Various Sizes

These are an invaluable aid to rescuing dropped stitches, undertaking a crochet cast on, or for adding a fancy edge to a project. Very small crochet hooks are required for beadwork. The smallest readily available size seems to be 0.6mm, however, it might be possible to find a 0.4mm with a bit of searching on the internet.

Stitch Markers or Waste Yarn to Use as Markers

These are essentially to help keep track of a pattern, and are particularly useful if you have a lot of stitches. Choose stitch markers that are not too heavy, that will not get tangled in your lace and that have rings that will not snag.

Safety Pins

These are useful for securing a dropped stitch until you are in a position to deal with it, or for using as a stitch holder for a very small amount of stitches.

Stitch Holders

These are used for holding stitches while they are not required, or being worked.

Measuring Tape and Ruler

These are useful for checking gauge on your swatches, the ruler is preferable for this as it provides greater accuracy, whereas for measuring larger items, a measuring tape will be the best option.

Waste Yarn

Waste yarn is useful for provisional cast ons, and for inserting as life lines to protect your work in case of error or lost stitches. I use a dye fast cotton or crochet thread in a contrasting colour, as it is a smooth, strong yarn and, especially for life lines, it makes seeing and picking up small stitches much easier. If using the top down construction method, waste yarn is very useful to thread your stitches on to so that you can try on the garment as you go to check the sizing.

Sewing Needles

Blunt-ended sewing needles, darning needles and wool needles with sharp points for sewing in ends, joining in yarns, inserting life lines and grafting.

Scissors for Snipping Ends

Small scissors are best for this as it is easy to catch your work with larger scissors with the resulting unwanted consequences.

Regular Graph Paper and Stitch-related Graph Paper

Regular graph paper is very useful for plotting a design on paper and for creating your own charts. Stitch-related graph paper has squares that have been elongated to emulate the shape of knit stitches. This is widely available online with the option to format the paper to match your stitch gauge. This is particularly useful if you want to get a clearer idea of how your stitches will relate to one another once knitted. Both types of graph paper are frequently free to download and print on the internet.

Lace Pins

These have bigger heads than regular pins and are an essential item for pinning out lace when blocking. T pins are particularly useful and are used with blocking wires to hold them in place.

You will need space to pin out your finished project. A traditional blocking frame is not necessary, although if you are going to knit a lot of lace these are very useful for larger projects. Lace can be blocked on mats or boards on the floor. Even bedspreads, towels or carpets can be used to pin your lace to if you don't have access to mats or boards.

Blocking Wires

Fine, flexible, rust- and tarnish-free wires are used to ensure that the lace is evenly stretched when using mats. These are threaded along the edges of the lace and across peaks in edgings and then pulled out by being pinned into position.

Yarns

There is a vast array of beautiful and tempting yarn available to the lace knitter. Both natural and synthetic along with innumerable blends and weights and textures, thus choosing the right yarn can be a challenge. When considering what kind of yarn to use for a project, it is helpful to have an understanding of how different types of yarn may perform when knitted as lace. Lace is routinely blocked after knitting in order to pull out the stitches and reveal the pattern. Some yarns will respond better to this than others.

For those wishing to knit fine airy lace, then lace weight and cobweb yarns will be your favoured option. However, not all lace weight yarns are the same; some may be lighter, some heavier, they may be tightly spun or loose but all may be described as lace weight. Then there are the cobweb weights, and the ultimate challenge for the lace knitter, the gossamer weights, very fine yarns, but again the actual fineness of these yarn weights will vary. To some extent it depends on whether you buy yarn specifically produced for the hand knitter, which may prove to be more consistent in weight, or hand spun yarn, which is likely to be more variable or whether you use coned yarns produced for machine knitting, and which can be bought as mill ends from commercial knitwear producers. These come in a wide variety of weights. The purchase of the latter is, however, an approach which can prove to be quite cost effective if you are a prodigious knitter, but can contribute to a significant tendency towards an excess of stash.

The weights of the mill end yarns are described differently to those used for commercially available hand knitting yarns. A system known as NM numbers is frequently used and this can be confusing if you are unfamiliar with this method of describing yarn weights. Essentially, the NM number describes how many metres will come from one gram of yarn. So, for example, a yarn described as having an NM of 1/28 will produce twenty-eight metres to the gram, whereas a yarn with an NM of 2/28 will produce half that amount, so fourteen metres to one gram. The figure 2 denotes that the yarn is twice as thick. As far as NM numbers are concerned, lace weight yarns are in the range of 1/14, 2/14, 2/28, 2/30 whilst a heavier lace weight would come in at 3/28. Another clue to the relative fineness of the yarn is the yardage. The more metres per 100 grams, the finer the yarn; so a fine lace weight yarn may produce in the region of 1,400 metres per 100 grams whereas a double knit might give you about 340 metres.

Sometimes you might see reference to WPI, wraps per inch. Lace weight yarns come into the range of 20–25 wraps per inch, very fine cobweb or gossamer weights could be as much forty wraps per inch. If you want to check the WPI of a yarn then it is simple enough to do, by wrapping the yarn evenly, without gaps, around something like a knitting needle or a pencil and then measuring the number of wraps per inch on a ruler.

Lace weight and cobweb yarns manufactured for hand knitting, as well as hand spun yarns, require no special treatment and can be swatched and then knitted straightaway. If, however, you choose to use the coned yarns from the mills then you will need to remember that it will probably be necessary to remove the commercial machine oils from your yarn by washing, either before you begin to knit, or afterwards. In the case of lace weight yarns, pre-washing before knitting is quite a challenge with infinite opportunities for the operation to result in a tangled mess! If you are determined to do so, then

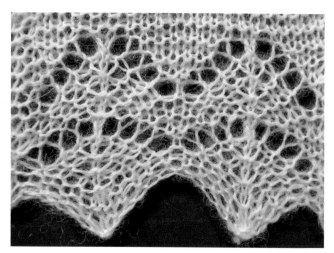

Horseshoe lace knitted in 100 per cent wool; Shetland Supreme 2 ply yarn, from Jamieson and Smith.

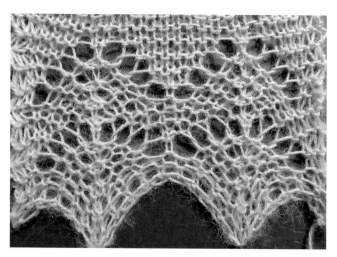

Horseshoe lace in heavy lace weight Blue Faced Leicester.

carefully skein the yarn, and secure it by tying firmly at very frequent intervals to avoid tangles whilst in the water, then follow the instructions in Chapter 8 on finishing techniques where this process is described for completed knitting projects. The method to be used is identical. In my experience, the better option is not to wash your yarn until after knitting. Whilst this may sound a little daunting it is remarkably simple to do.

Providing that you first knit your swatch, wash it according to the instructions, block it and then measure it, you will be able to calculate what your gauge should be, and can cast on the stitches required. Once your project is completed you can wash it and know what its size and gauge will be. You will also know how your finished piece will look, what the stitch definition and drape are like and know how it will react to blocking – all useful information in the creation of lace.

For the washing of commercial mill end yarns, please see the instructions in Chapter 8 – Finishing Techniques.

Types of Yarn

The following is not intended to provide a definitive list of all the very numerous types of yarn that are available and which are suitable for knitting lace. It does, however, provide an overview and some general information about the most commonly used yarns. There are many blends available, and yarns made from an assortment of unusual and interesting plant fibre. There is no reason at all why lace should not be knitted from almost any type of yarn that appeals to you. The advice is, as always, make a swatch first, before embarking on your project to test

how the yarn will perform in relation to your design, and in relation to the blocking process.

We will start with sheep's wool which is frequently used to knit lace. There are various types, for example, Shetland wool, Merino, and specific British breeds sheep. All of them will have different properties, some will be softer than others and some provide better stitch definition and drape than others.

Shetland Wool

Shetland wool, which is probably one of the first types of yarn to spring to mind when you think about knitting lace, provides good stitch definition and blocks extremely well. It is soft and warm, and creates beautiful extremely light and airy lace. Because wool is quite sticky, and Shetland is particularly so, it is easier to deal with dropped stitches than is the case with some other more slippery yarns.

Blue Faced Leicester

British breed sheep yarns are well worth experimenting with, and I particularly enjoy working with Blue Faced Leicester because of its softness and slightly fuzzy sheen. Again, it is yarn that blocks well and has good stitch definition.

Merino

Merino is a popular choice for lace. It is a soft warm yarn derived from a particular breed of sheep now generally found in Australia and New Zealand. It has good stitch definition and takes blocking well. It is not as crisp as Shetland wool but has a lovely drape and is easier to wear for those with sensitive skins. Extra fine Merino is spun using a special process to emulate

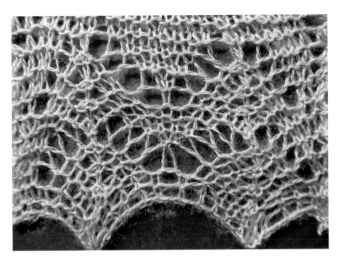

Horseshoe lace in lace weight Merino, from ColourMart.

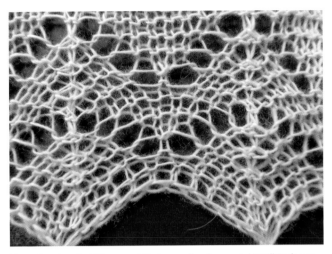

Horseshoe lace in 100 per cent Cashmere, fine lace weight Mill End yarn.

cashmere, often called Cashwool, and some of it is indeed as soft as any Cashmere. It is a beautiful yarn to work with, and creates a lovely, versatile and warm fabric.

Wool needs to washed with care, by hand, unless labelled as super wash in which case you might get away with a machine wash. Always test this first with a swatch.

Cashmere

Cashmere is derived from the soft down of the Kashmir goat. These goats are found in India, Tibet, Mongolia, Turkistan, Iran, Iraq and China. It is a beautiful, luxury yarn, and it has a lovely drape, is light and very warm, but it is not typically a strong yarn. Cashmere has much less memory than Shetland or Merino and is often blended with other yarns which improves its elasticity, strength and durability and creates beautifully soft blends, for example, Cashmere and Merino, with the Merino bringing the increased elasticity to the Cashmere, whilst the Cashmere adds softness and loft to the Merino. As with all yarn, not all Cashmere is created equal so swatching to see how it will perform is recommended. It is a yarn, however, that can create the most beautiful and warm lace, and is soft next to the skin and a truly luxurious fabric.

Alpaca

Alpacas produce a yarn that is soft, sturdier than Cashmere and lighter than sheep wool. It is an extremely warm yarn and is also used for lace. Alpaca lacks the elasticity of wool and although it will stretch, it has less 'ping' and will not spring back quite as readily. Alpaca has a lovely drape and lustre, often with a halo when knitted. Swatching is advised before embarking on

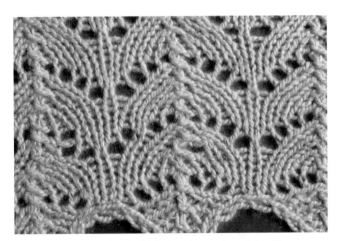

Horseshoe lace knitted in double knit cashmere, from ColourMart.

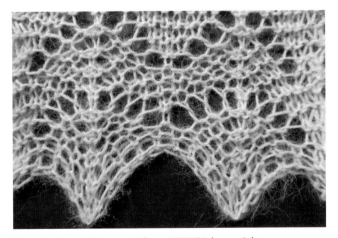

Horseshoe lace. 100 per cent Alpaca, NM 2/28, lace weight, from ColourMart.

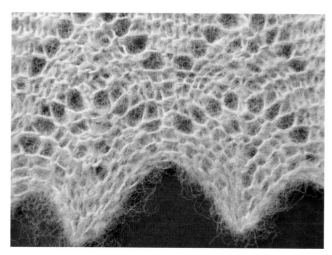

Horseshoe lace in lace weight Kid Mohair. See how fuzzy the motif is in this yarn.

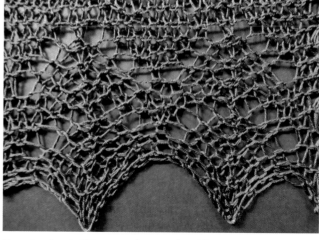

Horseshoe lace in 100 per cent lace weight wild silk, from ColourMart.

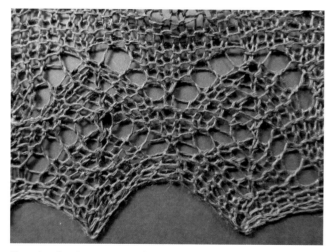

Horseshoe lace in 100 per cent linen, very fine lace weight.

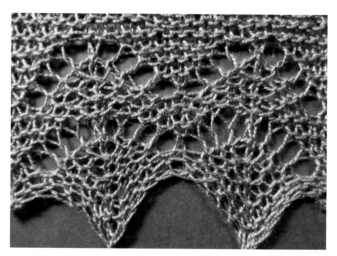

Horseshoe lace in 100 per cent lace weight cotton.

any project to check how the yarn will react to the pattern and the blocking process.

Mohair

Mohair comes from the Angora goat. It is a light and airy yarn which knits up with a distinct halo, and creates beautiful lace. It can, however, be quite hairy which would be an issue for those with sensitive skin, despite its apparent softness. The halo that is created when mohair is knitted can obscure the pattern of the lace if care is not taken to manage the size of needles and the stitch that is to be used. Kid Mohair and blends with silk are very popular, particularly for lace as the silk tends to reduce the extent of the halo as well as adding strength to the yarn.

Silk

Silk is a strong yarn that takes blocking very well, it is not an elastic yarn, and whilst it does have drape and sheen, it can drop if the tension is too loose, so swatching to make sure that the yarn is producing an effective fabric for your project is essential.

Silk is often blended with other fibre, for example, cotton and silk work well together, as do silk and linen and silk and wool. All will work well for lace.

Cotton and Linen

Cotton and linen are both strong yarns and can be used to produce very crisp lace. Linen can be hard on the hands and may not feel like a joy to knit but can produce beautiful finished

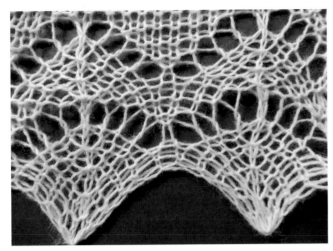

Horseshoe lace in a fine lace weight cotton Cashmere blend.

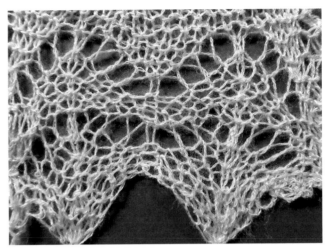

Horseshoe lace in 100 per cent lace weight Cashmere sparkle yarn from ColourMart. A touch of luxury and sparkle in this lovely blend.

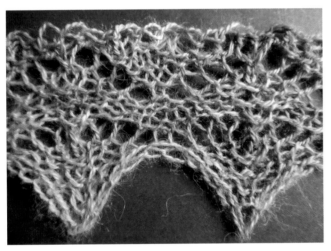

Horseshoe lace in Manos Del Uruguay, Baby Alpaca 70 per cent, silk 25 per cent and Cashmere 5 per cent.

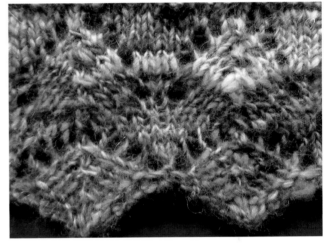

Horseshoe lace in handspun yarn from Gongcrafts in the far north of Scotland.

results. Linen tends to soften over time with washing. Both cotton and linen work beautifully when blended with other fibre, and a cotton Cashmere, or linen silk blend for lace can create a strong, but light and warm fabric, ideal for summer garments or floaty romantic shawls.

Blends

There are many blends and weights of yarn available, all of which will give beautiful results for lace and it is fun to experiment with different types to see what effect will be created. A cotton cashmere blend is a particularly good example of this.

Sparkle yarns which are now widely available can create really beautiful lace. It is also possible to add a lurex thread to your lace yarn if you wish, thus making your own customized sparkle yarn for a project.

Not all lace has to be knitted in lace weight or cobweb weight. It is perfectly possible to knit lace with any weight of yarn if you want, so for example, a lacy scarf in a double knit or even an Aran weight yarn is perfectly feasible, the result being largely down to the fabric that can be achieved, the lace pattern chosen and adjusting the size of the needles accordingly. Some stunning effects can be achieved by using gradient yarns for lace projects. Sock yarns are often a good choice if you want to experiment with this approach, although there are now many dyed and hand painted yarns available specifically aimed at the lace knitter.

CHAPTER 3

TECHNIQUES

In order to knit lace, you will need to be able to knit, purl, perform yarn over increases and knit 2 and 3 together decreases as a basic skill set. In addition, you will need to be able to follow and understand written patterns and charts.

Increasing

Yarn-Over Increase

A yarn-over increase is used to create a hole, and is paired with a corresponding decrease. To execute this on a knit row, bring the yarn under the right-hand needle to the front of the work, as if to purl, then bring the yarn over the top of the right-hand needle and knit the next stitch on the left-hand needle. One stitch increased.

To increase a stitch purlwise, bring the yarn over the top of the right-hand needle and back under the needle to the front, and purl the next stitch: one stitch increased.

Other Increases

Knit Front and Back (kfb)

This increase is used where you want an almost invisible increase, for example, along a seam line in a knitted garment. To perform this, increase the knit into the stitch as if to knit but do not slip the stitch off, then knit into the back of the stitch, before slipping the stitch off.

Make 1 Left. (M1L)

This increase is almost invisible and is useful where obvious signs of increase are not wanted.

Using the left-hand needle, insert it from front to back under the thread that runs between the next stitch and the last stitch that you worked on the right-hand needle and place it on the left-hand needle.

Now knit this through the back of the loop.

This produces a left leaning slant.

Make 1 Right. (M1R)

Using the left-hand needle, insert it from back to front under the thread that runs between the next stitch and the last stitch that you worked on the right-hand needle and place it on the left-hand needle.

Knit through the front of the loop.

This creates a right leaning increase.

Decreasing

Knit 2 Together (k2tog)
This is probably the best-known decrease and produces a slant to the right. Insert the right-hand needle knitwise into the next two stitches on the left-hand needle and knit them together. The decrease slopes to the right.

Purl 2 Together (p2tog)
Insert the right-hand needle purlwise into the next two stitches on the left-hand needle purlwise and purl them together. Decrease slopes to the right.

Knit 2 Together Through the Back of the Loop (k2tog tbl)
This and the following decreases all produce a left leaning slant so it is useful to balance the k2tog decreases. Insert the right-hand needle into the back of the next two stitches on the left-hand needle and knit them together. This gives a slant to the left.

Purl 2 Together Through the Back of the Loop (p2tog tbl)
Insert the right-hand needle into the back of the next two purl stitches and purl them together. The slant leans to the left.

Slip, Slip, Knit (ssk)
Slip the next two stitches knitwise, one after the other, to the right-hand needle. Bring the yarn over the right-hand needle and with the left needle, lift the stitches over the yarn. The slant leans to the left.

As an alternative, ssk can be knitted as follows: slip the first stitch knitwise, the second stitch purlwise, and then complete as above.

Slip 1, Knit 1, Pass Slip Stitch Over (skp)
Slip a stitch, then knit the next stitch and pass the slipped stitch over it. The slant leans to the left.

Casting On

There are various methods of casting on and most of us will have our particular favourite. Many of the methods more generally used will give a firm cast on edge which doesn't work particularly well with lace so it needs a looser stretchy edging to allow the lace to be opened up when blocked. If the edge is too firm it draws the lace in and spoils the look.

Lace Cast On
This cast on is also known as a knitted on cast on. It produces a loose stretchy cast on with a line of loops, which are easy to see and pick up if you need to attach an edging later.

To perform this cast on, leave a tail of 5–8cm, and make a slip knot, which you place on your left-hand needle. Now insert your right-hand needle into the stitch as if to knit, wind the wool around the needle and pull the needle through the loop, again exactly as if you are knitting the stitch. Instead of slipping the stitch off the needle, slip it onto the left-hand needle, one stitch cast on. Now insert your right-hand needle into the new stitch as if to knit and repeat the process, placing each new stitch onto the left-hand needle until the required number of stitches have been cast on.

Note the difference between the lace cast on on the right and the regular cast on edge on the left.

Provisional Cast On

This cast on provides for a line of live stitches to be accessible to be picked up later in the project. This allows for an invisible join when knitting on an edging at the end of the project.

To do this you will need a length of waste yarn. Using your preferred method, cast on the required amount of stitches, knit two or three rows and then join in the yarn for the project.

When you want to access the live stitches later on, carefully unpick the waste yarn.

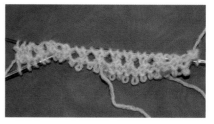

Pick up the live stitches and replace them on your needle, ready to knit.

Crochet Cast On

Alternatively, another method of producing a line of live stitches for use later on is a crochet cast on.

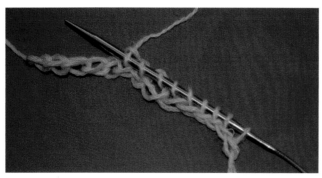

Using a length of waste yarn, make a line of chain stitches with your crochet hook, ensuring that you have sufficient loops for the number of stitches required. With your knitting needle, pick up and knit into each of the loops for the requisite number of stitches.

Later when you need to access the live stitches, carefully unravel the crochet stitches whilst picking up the live stitches from each loop and placing them onto your needle ready to work.

Thumb or Loop Method

This method can provide a lovely, loose and even cast on for lace.

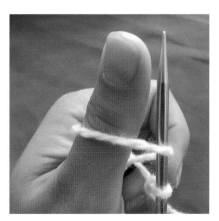

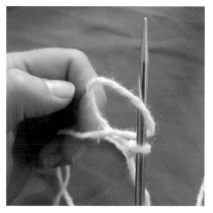

Make a slip knot a few centimetres from the end of the yarn. Next, whilst holding the needle with the loop on it in your right hand, take the yarn from the ball in your left hand, pass it over the top of your thumb from front to back.

Insert right-hand needle knitwise into the yarn on the front of your thumb.

Pull the tail tight whilst slipping stitch onto the right-hand needle, one stitch made.

Continue in this manner until a sufficient number of stitches have been cast on. Again, this cast on provides a loose, stretchy cast on with loops that can be accessed for knitting on an edging later if desired.

Picot Cast On

This cast on method provides an attractive edging useful for cuffs and bands. It can be matched with a picot cast off.

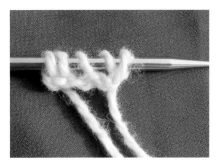

Make a slip knot and place it on the left-hand needle. Next cast on four stitches using the knitted-on method (*see* above). You now have five stitches on your needle.

Knit two stitches from left-hand needle and cast off one stitch.

Knit the next stitch and cast off one stitch.

Place the remaining stitch from the right-hand needle onto left hand needle. You should now have three stitches on the left-hand needle.

Cast on four more stitches as before, and then knit and cast off two as before, transferring the third back to the left-hand needle.

Continue in this manner until you have the required number of stitches.

Cable Cast On

This cast on gives a much firmer edge and occasionally this might be just what you want at the start of your project.

Make a slip knot and place it on the left-hand needle. Knit into the stitch and slip the stitch made onto the left-hand needle without slipping it off, as in the lace cast on. Now insert the right-hand needle behind the last stitch made, so it is between the two stitches on the left-hand needle. Wrap the yarn around the needle as if knitting the stitch, pull the loop through and place the stitch on the left-hand needle. One stitch cast on. Now insert the right-hand needle behind the last stitch cast on and repeat until the required number of stitches have been cast on.

Casting off

Lace Cast Off

For lace knitting, a standard cast off often appears too rigid and like the firmer cast on techniques, it can draw in your work and potentially spoil the appearance of the finished article by pulling the lace out of shape. There are, however, some techniques to counter this. One method is to cast off in the usual way but to use a needle a size or two larger. Whilst this produces a looser edge, this can still feel rather rigid and looks different to the airiness of the lace cast on. To counter this and in order to achieve a stretchy cast off that provides a closer match to the lace cast on in appearance, try using the following technique.

Knit the first stitch, yarn over, knit the second stitch, slip the first stitch and the yarn over together over the second stitch knitted as you would in a regular cast off, one stitch cast off, but you have a loop and no tightness. Continue in this manner until all the stitches have been cast off. The same technique can be applied to a purl cast off. Visually you now have a cast-off edge that is not identical but more closely mirrors that of your cast on edge, which produces a much more satisfactory finish.

Picot Cast Off

This technique produces an attractive edging and the frequency of the picot points can be as varied as you wish.

In order to achieve this cast off, use the cable cast on method to cast on two, three, four or more stitches depending on how big you want your picots to be, then immediately cast them off.

Pass the remaining stitch back to the left-hand needle and use it to cast on the next batch of stitches for the picot, or depending on how closely spaced you wish your picots to be, cast off one or more stitches before cable casting on for the next picot.

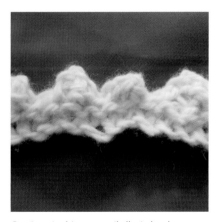

Continue in this way until all stitches have been cast off.

Inserting a Life Line

The insertion of a life line provides you with an emergency safety system by catching lost stitches or allowing you to unravel all your stitches back to a point in your work where you know that everything was accurate. It is exactly what it says on the tin – a life line!

Some circular needles include holes for the insertion of life lines; however, failing that, life lines are very easy to insert, and much to be recommended. You can literally save yourself many hours of work and considerable frustration if something has gone wrong and you have to take your work back or rescue a dropped stitch.

Always insert a life line at a point in your knitting where you know that everything is right. You might find it helpful, for example, to insert life lines at the end of a pattern repeat where you are absolutely certain that there are no mistakes or missing stitches. By always putting the life line in at the end of a pattern repeat, you will always know which row you are starting with if you have to take the work back to the life line.

Take a length of smooth contrasting waste yarn, thread it onto a blunt ended needle and then carefully thread the needle through each of the stitches, without removing them from the needle. Make sure that you catch each stitch. It is important to ensure that the waste yarn is long enough not to start slipping back along the row as you knit.

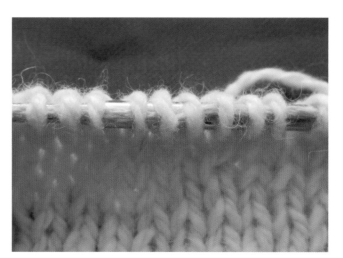

Life line inserted through all the stitches.

Joining in Yarn

It is generally taught that to join a yarn by knotting is a serious knitting sin and that you should therefore endeavour to avoid this. Sometimes, however, securing yarn at the edges of your knitting by making a knot, especially with very fine yarn can be an acceptable solution, but make sure that it is secure and then sew in the ends afterwards. Knots in the middle of rows, especially in lace knitting, do not work and are very difficult to hide unless you can make them disappear into a decrease or a bobble. It is useful sometimes to knot yarns at a join with a view to unknotting them later to sew in. If you do this make sure you leave long enough ends.

It is preferable wherever possible to try and join in new yarn at the edge of your knitting or to use one of the following methods if joining mid row is required or if you simply do not want any ends to sew in. If you are joining in yarn at the edge of the work, ensure you leave a long enough tail for it to be neatly sewn in at the completion of the work.

If you need to join in a new yarn of the same colour either mid row, or at the edge of your work and you want to avoid any loose ends then one of the following methods can be quite effective.

Spit Splicing

Spit splicing is probably the most effective method, the least visible and is very simple to do. However, this method only works on animal fibres.

It is possible to use this method to join a new colour but there will be an obvious area of yarn mixing at the join, which again may not be an acceptable option depending upon your project.

A final word about spit splicing, it can also be done using water although it is often suggested that spit provides a stronger join!

There are alternative options for joining in a new colour mid row or when knitting in the round.

Take the ends of both your working yarn and your new yarn.

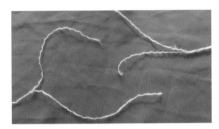

Unravel the plies for an inch or so.

Divide the plies evenly and snip off half on both lengths of yarn. So, if your yarn has four plies then you will snip off two of the plies from both your working and your new yarn. You are left with two lengths of yarn each, with two plies.

Now lay the remaining plies against each other with their ends overlapping and apply spit.

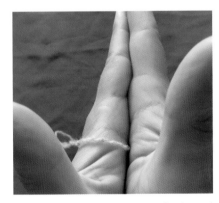

Rub between your hands, creating friction and heat, which effectively felts the ends together.

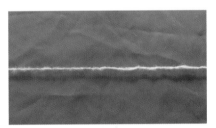

This creates a strong and almost completely invisible join with the only possible issue being that the felted yarn will have a slightly stiffer feel.

Loop Join

The first involves knitting to the point where the colour change or yarn change is to happen.

This works well with any type of yarn, both synthetic and natural fibres.

The beauty of this method is that you are left with no ends to sew in and although there is a thickening where the double thickness of the loops is knitted, it is not very obvious unless you have used this method on very fine open work, in which case it may not be the most effective option.

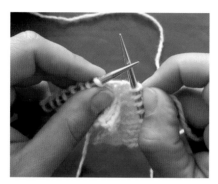

Pinch your working yarn between your thumb and forefinger against the last complete stitch.

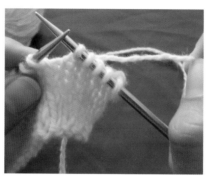

Now carefully unpick the last three or four stitches whilst continuing to hold on to the yarn.

Next fold the yarn from the point at which you are holding it to form a loop.

Take the new yarn or colour and thread the end through the loop and double the new yarn to make a similar loop.

Now knit the double strand of the loop with the original working yarn.

Then continue with the double strand of the new working yarn for a few stitches until it is secure.

Then continue with the single thread.

A neat join but leaves a step. This is not an issue if joining in a same colour yarn.

Russian Join

There is a variation on this technique known as the Russian join. Again, this is a join that is effective across all types of fibres. In order to make the Russian join you will need a sharp needle.

The advantage of this join is that it is easy to join in a new colour without creating holes or loose ends. However, there is a thickening of the yarn, which on finer work may not be as invisible as you might wish.

On the basis that there is no perfect method for joining in new yarns, you will need to decide on which method will provide the least obvious join, depending upon the nature of your project and the type of yarn you are using.

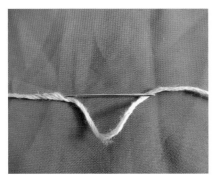

Thread your working yarn through the needle, loosen the plies and then thread the needle through the centre of the yarn.

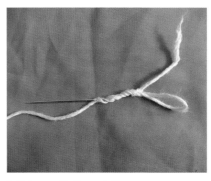

Pull the needle through the yarn.

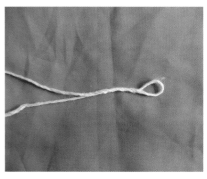

Make sure that you leave a loop at the top as you pull the needle through.

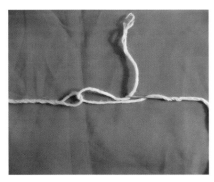

Now thread the new yarn through the needle, draw the new yarn through the loop you left on the working yarn, then loosening the plies on the new yarn, thread the needle through the centre of the new yarn.

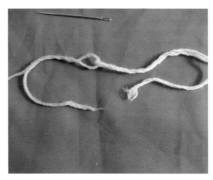

Remove the needle and pull on the short ends of both yarns to tighten the loop.

Now snip the loose ends.

Knitting on Edges

If you are going to knit on an edge to your project, it is helpful to plan this in advance. If you are adding a lace edging to a garment then you are in effect replacing the rib or other border with a lace edge.

If you are knitting a traditional button up cardigan, consider using a provisional cast on and then pick up the stitches for the front bands and neck just as you would for a regular rib band, and knit the bottom border and the front bands in one.

If you are knitting a top down cardigan, you will reach the bottom and have live stitches on your needle. You can then pick up the front band and neck stitches and again knit your lace edge on in one go.

To knit on a lace edging to a scarf or wrap, you will most likely have used a provisional cast on.

You can plot the placement of the edging against the main pattern stitches by using squared paper. If possible try and centre the edging pattern so it looks more balanced. This may mean that you start halfway through the pattern repeat in order to get the pattern to centre and to be balanced and mirrored on the ends. This is something that you can experiment with when you knit your swatch.

Knit your wrap/scarf until it is the size and dimensions that you require.

Continue in this manner until one stitch remains on the left-hand needle.

On the next wrong side row, cast off the edge stitches (either very loosely or using a lace cast off) in the normal manner until one stitch remains on the left-hand needle and one stitch remains on the right-hand needle. Knit these stitches together and fasten off.

Ending with a right-side row, turn your work and cast on the required number of stitches for your edging using a lace cast on. Cast on stitches for edging are seen in grey.

With the wrong side facing you, work back to the main stitches and knit the last cast on stitch together with the first stitch on the left-hand needle.

Turn the work, slip the first stitch then start your lace pattern.

At the end of the row, turn your work and work back, making sure that you knit the last edge stitch together with the first stitch on the left-hand needle on this and every wrong side row.

Working with Charts

Not all lace patterns come with a written set of instructions so having a basic grasp of how charts work (even if they are not your preferred option of pattern) is very useful.

Many people find understanding and following charts very difficult and prefer to stick with a written-out pattern. On the basis that there are no knitting police, there is nothing wrong with this approach and if it works for you then you may see little value in trying to understand and use charts. However, as mentioned above not all lace patterns come with a written down set of instructions so if you are unable to work from a chart or interpret it, you may lose the opportunity to knit a pattern that you are drawn to. On the other hand, you may be frustrated and not a little daunted in your efforts to get to grips with this method of following a pattern having heard fellow knitters saying how much easier they find using the charts to the written down patterns.

It can be easy to get lost in a long list of written instructions, and for many people once they have been introduced to using charts, they soon come to prefer this method to the written pattern. If you are a visual person you will find it really helpful to be able to see a pictorial representation of what your stitches should be doing and how they relate to one another. It can be challenging the first time you are confronted with a chart, and it can prove quite a struggle and very frustrating to make sense of it if you do not have an explanation as to how to proceed. The following paragraphs aim to bring some clarity to those of you grappling with the chart challenge.

Learning to use charts feels a little like trying to learn to read a new language comprised of symbols. To complicate matters further, the reading of this language is from the bottom right corner of the page rather than the top left which is the way that most of us would generally expect to proceed. However, it is not nearly as complicated as it might first appear.

When you look at a chart you are confronted with symbols on a grid. These indicate the way in which the pattern is be to knitted. Just to add further complications, in the knitting world there is no unified series of symbols, and these can and do vary from designer to designer, depending on their preference, and in some cases, their use of their own unique set of charting symbols, providing a further challenge to the knitter. To help you, each chart comes with a key, interpreting the symbols contained within the chart.

If you look at a chart, what you are seeing is essentially a visual image of your knit stitches reduced to squares on a sheet of paper. When you are knitting you knit the stitches from the left-hand needle onto the right-hand needle. The chart is in effect your left-hand needle, with all your stitches lined up ready to be knitted. Read the chart as you knit, so for all flat knitting read the chart from the bottom up, and from right to left for the first row and then left to right for the second row and so forth.

Starting in the right-hand corner on row one, stitch one, with the right side of your knitting facing you, knit each stitch according to the symbol contained in the square. The chart shows you which bit of the pattern is the repeat, the bit in the red frame in this book, which is the same as the bit that you see between stars and brackets in a written pattern, and it sets out the first few stitches and the final few stitches that you need to complete the start and finish of the row. Again, these are the start and finish stitches that you see in your written pattern. Repeat the main pattern as many times as indicated in the pattern, and conclude the row with the final few stitches. (*See* diagram below.)

The arrows indicate the direction of knit for each row. Start where indicated in the bottom right hand corner. Slip the first stitch, k5, yo, sl, k2tog, psso, yo, k to the end of the row. Turn your work and slip the first stitch, then purl back across to the end of the row.

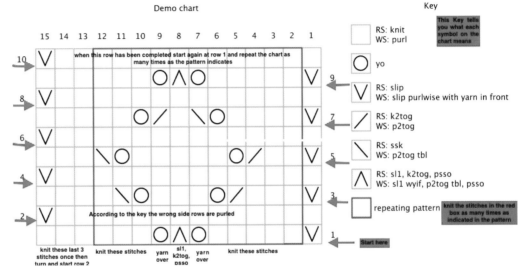

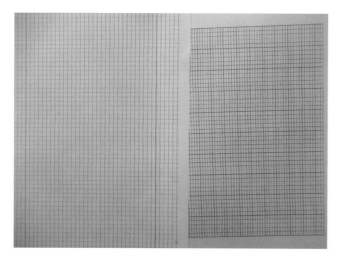

This shows the difference between regular graph paper on the left and stitch related graph paper on the right.

For your next row, the wrong side row, start at the left-hand side of the chart, again knitting each stitch in accordance with the symbol contained in the squares. If there are no symbols then either knit or purl back to the end of the row ready to start on the next right-side row on the right-hand side of the chart. Anything that is unusual, or if there are any special stitch techniques, should be explained in the instructions for the pattern.

For knitting in the round the approach is slightly different, and whilst the chart still starts in the bottom right hand corner, it is read from right to left on all rows, again to emulate the circular nature of the knitting. The interpretation of the symbols continues to be explained in the key.

Some charts contain stitches that are not there: the 'no stitch' squares. This can be confusing if you have not come across this before, but simply ignore them; on that row they do not exist, probably because they have been decreased and therefore cease to exist for the time being and will be replaced in a few rows' time.

One of the main advantages of a chart is that it is easy to see the pattern and to see how stitches relate to one another. It is also easier to see where you are if you have a pictorial representation of the stitches in front of you rather than trying to establish which part of a written instruction you have got to and which you should be knitting next. It is easy to keep track of your place on a chart, either by placing a ruler above or below the row you are knitting, or using Post-it notes or similar to mark your place.

Being able to use charts is an invaluable aid to plotting your own designs, and provides an opportunity to get down on paper ideas for how motifs, edgings and insertions might work together. It is easy to adjust an edge, a stitch or insertion on a chart and see straightaway how this affects the rest of your design. It could be argued that without at least a basic understanding of charting, the opportunities to create your own designs will be much more difficult to execute.

It is perfectly possible to create charts for lace knitting on regular squared paper; however, there is graph paper available that has been specifically designed for the knitter.

Knit related graph paper is a little different from regular graph paper in that the squares are more rectangular and are thus more stitch shaped than regular graph paper squares. This may not matter very much when you are simply trying to rough out a design; however, if you are wanting to get a better idea of how to obtain a particular result, having graph paper that is the same scale as your knitted swatch can be very helpful.

As previously indicated, this is widely available and for the most part it is free to download and print on the internet. You are prompted to generate your own scaled paper by entering the stitch and row gauge according to the knitted tension swatch. The paper is then generated to match the dimensions of your knitted swatch.

Swatching

And finally, to the often contentious and already frequently-mentioned topic of swatching. I know that many people find it a chore and will avoid knitting a swatch if at all possible. Nevertheless, the importance of swatching cannot be over emphasized. If you pick up a pattern and use the needles indicated it is more likely than not that the finished result will be too big, too small or not the shape that you were expecting, which is very disappointing. The difficulty here is that no two people have the same tension when they are knitting, so the designer who produced the pattern will indicate the tension that worked for them and to which the pattern was designed. Therefore, in order to replicate the pattern, it is important that the *basic gauge* rather than the needle size is the same as the original used by the designer. This may require some trial and re-knitting with different sized needles before beginning the project to make sure you get the gauge that is required but it is well worth the effort. To have spent time and money on a project that then fails can be very discouraging and may make the difference between someone persevering with a project or abandoning it, or even giving up knitting altogether. There may of course be occasions when the exact dimensions of your project may not be that important, for example, in the Hap throw later in this book.

However the look, the feel and the texture of your fabric will matter, and it is not possible to know how this will look unless you have knitted and blocked a swatch before beginning your project. This is so important with lace, whereby having knitted your swatch you might discover that the yarn biases, for example, or is not very strong and breaks when being blocked. It is so much better to decide on a change of yarn, needle size or general approach before you start, rather than at the end of, or even halfway through a piece of work, with the inevitable result of needing to take it back and start again.

Generally you should start by knitting a swatch a little bigger than 10cm × 10cm (4in × 4in) as gauge is usually calculated on the basis of × number of stitches to × number of rows to 10cm (4in). If you know this basic measurement you will be able to calculate the finished size of an item or garment and if following a pattern, in the knowledge that your gauge is accurate, you will have the great satisfaction of producing an item that is as you expected in terms of size, shape and fit.

To calculate your gauge, first block your swatch so that you have the finished measurements. Using a ruler placed across the middle of the swatch, count how many stitches there are to 10cm/4in. Note this down. Then place the ruler vertically across the middle of the swatch and count how many rows you have to 10cm/4in. Note this down. You now have the figures you need for your stitch × row gauge. Make sure you keep a note of the needle size used so that it is easy to replicate this stitch gauge later on.

If you manage to keep more or less to the same size for your swatches, why not use them to make a sampler of your own by joining together the squares. Most knitters can easily generate enough swatches to produce a patchwork throw or two, so nothing need ever be wasted.

A few of the swatches generated during the creation of this book.

CHAPTER 4

STITCHIONARY

This chapter contains charts, written instructions and images of lace motifs, as well as insertions, edgings and border stitches. Although there may seem to be a large number of patterns, in reality this is only a fraction of the lace patterns that exist. There are many patterns that are very similar, or even the same, or that have the same name but are in fact completely different from one another. I have tried to use the names most commonly associated with the patterns, and have included additional names where it seems helpful to do so. Some of the pattern charts appear similar to one another but the knitted results often look quite different. These similarities give a bit of an insight into the ways in which motifs may have developed over the years.

The aim of this chapter is to provide a sufficient number of motifs and options to allow for exploration of and experimentation with design and composition. I have endeavoured to select a variety of patterns with both interest and varying levels of difficulty. You will find that none are especially difficult and all use the yarn over increase and the knit 2 together or knit 3 together decreases that you are familiar with. The techniques are explained in the key that accompanies each of the charts. Whilst you will no doubt find some of the patterns very straightforward, there are some that require a little more concentration than others.

All of these motifs have been knitted in a cobweb weight Shetland wool from Jamieson and Smith on 3mm needles.

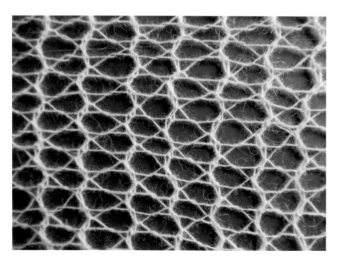

Vertical Trellis Faggot stitch.

Faggot Stitch

We start with this simple but useful stitch as it crops up frequently in lace, acting as a filler, providing borders and divisions between other motifs, as a basic pattern in edgings and can be used to great effect as a stand-alone all over pattern.

It is a lace constructed by alternating yarn overs and knit 2 togethers repeatedly across the row, and the arrangements of the repetitions of the knit 2 togethers, either left or right leaning and the placement of the yarn over is what provides the balance.

If the yarn over comes before the decrease stitch knit 2 together, the work will bias to the right, and if the yarn over comes after the decrease stitch slip knit pass slip stitch over (skp), it will bias to the left. Therefore, to obtain balance, work one row as yarn over, knit 2 together, right leaning slant, and the next as slip, knit, pass slip stitch over, left leaning slant, and then the yarn over. Vertical Trellis Faggot stitch uses this method and places a purl row between the faggot rows, thus providing a balanced fabric.

Vertical Trellis Faggot Stitch Instructions
Cast on an odd number of stitches.

Row 1: k1, (yo, k2tog) to end of row.
Row 2: Purl.
Row 3: (Skp, yo) repeat to end of row.
Row 4: Purl.
Repeat these 4 rows.

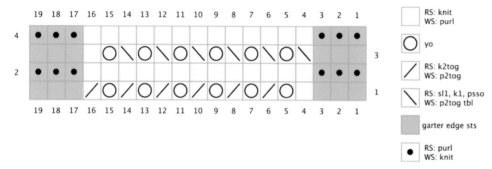

Vertical Trellis Faggot stitch chart.

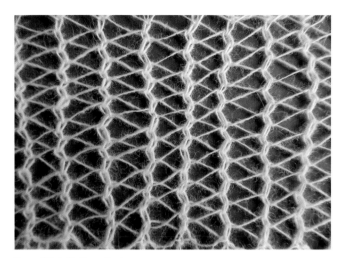

Purse Stitch (knit version).

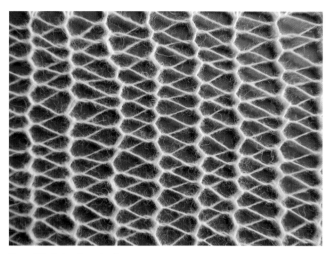

Purse Stitch (purl version).

Purse Stitch

Purse Stitch gained its name as it was used in the past to knit fine silk purses.

Purse Stitch Instructions
Cast on an even number of stitches.

Row 1: p1 (yo, p2tog), repeat to last stitch p1.
Repeat this row.

Alternately this can be knitted as follows:

Cast on an even number of stitches.

Row 1: k1, (yo, skp) to last stitch, k1.
Repeat this row.

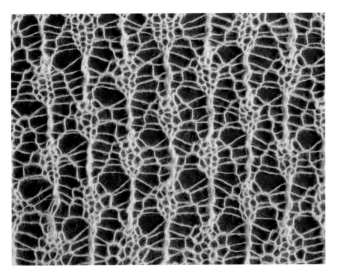

Madeira Mesh.

Madeira Mesh

Madeira Mesh is a very old pattern, possibly one of the earliest known lace patterns, which is said to be Spanish in origin. Compare this pattern to some of the other lace motifs in this stitchionary, for example, Fir Cone and Broken Acre particularly, and you will begin to see how lace may have developed. Take a look at Fir Cone and you can see that simply by changing the

spacing between the yarn over increases and knit 3 together decreases, that the pattern has changed completely. Despite its great age, Madeira Mesh is a lovely all over pattern although not commonly seen in modern day lace knitting. It is a very easy pattern to knit having a six stitch and twelve row repeat. The construct uses knit 3 together decreases and yarn overs separated by three knit stitches. At row six the pattern is moved across so that the yarn overs and knit 3 together decreases are now happening on the stitches that were previously knit stitches. Although the pattern is very simple, a chart is included as this illustrates very clearly the way in which the decrease stitches and the yarn overs shift at row 7.

Madeira Mesh Instructions
Cast on multiples of 6 stitches + 7.

Row 1 (RS): K2, (yo, sl1, k2tog, psso, yo, k3) × 2, yo, sl1, k2tog, psso, yo, k2. (19 sts)

Row 2 (WS): K2, (yo, sl1, k2tog, psso, yo, k3) × 2, yo, sl1, k2tog, psso, yo, k2.

Rows 3–6: Repeat rows 1–2.

Row 7: K5, yo, sl1, k2tog, psso, yo, k3, yo, sl1, k2tog, psso, yo, k5.

Row 8: K5, yo, sl1, k2tog, psso, yo, k3, yo, sl1, k2tog, psso, yo, k5.

Rows 9–12: Repeat rows 7–8.

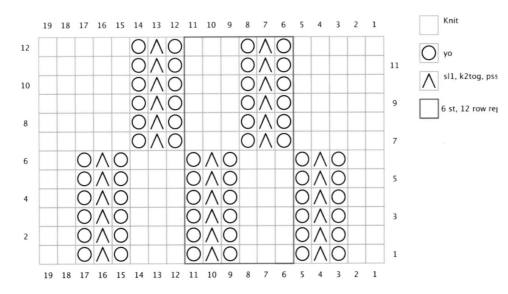

Madeira Mesh chart.

Acre Lace

This is generally described as a traditional Shetland motif, depicting a ploughed acre. It is knitted with a garter stitch ground.

Acre Lace Instructions
Multiples of 10 st.

Row 1 and all RS rows: Sl, k3, (k2tog, yo, k2, yo, ssk, k4) × 2.
Row 2 and all WS rows: Sl, k23.

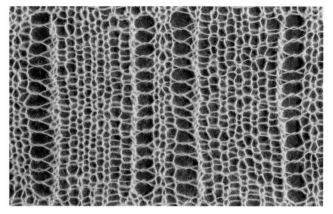

Acre Lace.

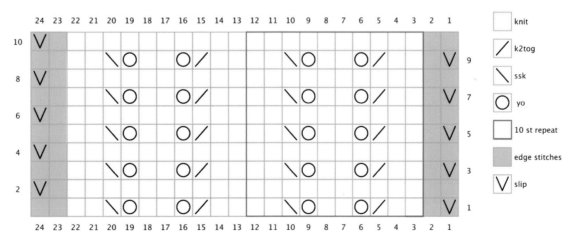

Acre Lace chart.

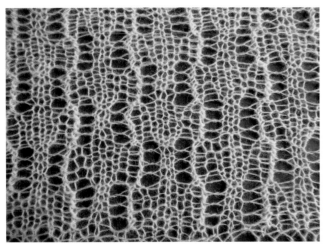

Broken Acre Lace.

Broken Acre

Broken Acre as you can see is Acre lace in an alternating pattern repeat. This gives a very pretty pattern and an attractive option for socks, lacy gloves or scarves. This is knitted with a garter stitch ground.

Broken Acre Instructions

Row 1 (RS): Sl, (k4, k2tog, yo, k2, yo, ssk) × 2, k5. (26 sts)

Row 2 and all WS rows: Sl, k25.

Row 3: Repeat row 1.

Row 5: Repeat row 1.

Row 7: Repeat row 1.

Row 9: Sl, k3, yo, ssk, k4, k2tog, yo, k2, yo, ssk, k4, k2tog, yo, k4.

Row 11: Repeat row 9.

Row 13: Repeat row 9.

Row 15: Repeat row 9.

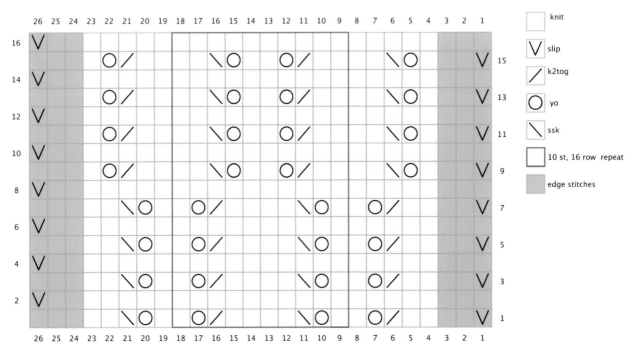

Broken Acre Lace chart.

	knit
V	slip
/	k2tog
O	yo
\	ssk
	10 st, 16 row repeat
	edge stitches

Birds Eye Lace

This is an attractive motif, and easy to see how it came to have its name. This requires a little more concentration than some of the motifs, being patterned on both the right and wrong side rows, but is well worth the endeavour. This is knitted in garter stitch.

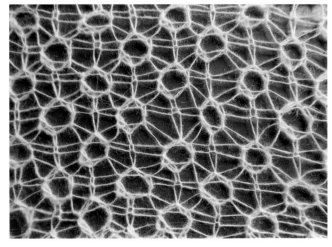

Birds Eye Lace.

Birds Eye Lace Instructions
Multiples of 6 + 13.

Row 1: Sl, k2, ssk, yo, k3, yo, sl1, k2tog, psso, yo, k3, yo, k2tog, k3. (19 sts)

Row 2: Sl, k3, yo, k2tog, k, ssk, yo, k, yo, k2tog, k, ssk, yo, k3, sl.

Row 3: Sl, k3, yo, ssk, yo, sl1, k2tog, psso, yo, k, yo, ssk, yo, sl1, k2tog, psso, yo, k4.

Row 4: Repeat row 2.

Row 5: Sl, k4, yo, sl1, k2tog, psso, yo, k3, yo, sl1, k2tog, psso, yo, k5.

Row 6: Sl, k3, ssk, yo, k, yo, k2tog, k, ssk yo, k, yo, k2tog, k4.

Row 7: Sl, k2, (yo, sl1, k2tog, psso, yo, k, yo, ssk) × 2, k4.

Row 8: Repeat row 6.

Row 9: Repeat row 1.

Row 10: Repeat row 2.

Row 11: Repeat row 3.

Row 12: Repeat row 2.

Row 13: Repeat row 5.

Row 14: Repeat row 6.

Row 15: Sl, k2, yo, sl1, k2tog, psso, (yo, k) × 2, yo, sl1, k2tog, psso, yo, k, yo, ssk, k4.

Row 16: Repeat row 6.

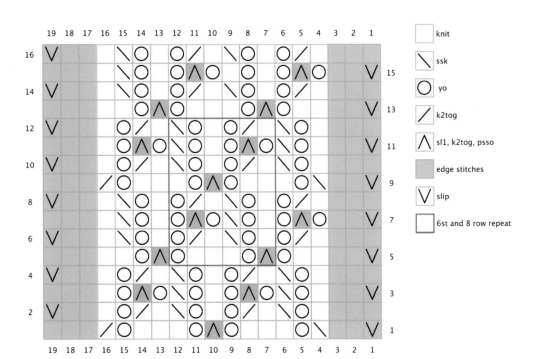

Birds Eye Lace chart.

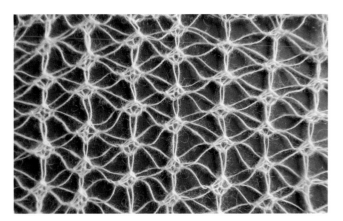

Bead Lace.

Bead Lace

This is a very attractive motif, but one that does require some concentration to complete, being patterned on both the right and wrong side rows. It makes a beautiful all over pattern or can alternatively be used to create diamond motifs. This sample is knitted in garter stitch.

Bead Lace Instructions

Row 1 (RS): Sl, k3, yo, ssk, k, k2tog, yo, k, yo, ssk, k, k2tog, yo, k4. (19 sts)

Row 2 (WS): Sl, k4, yo, sl1, k2tog, psso, yo, k3, yo, sl1, k2tog, psso, yo, k5.

Row 3: Sl, k3, k2tog, yo, k, yo, ssk, k, k2tog, yo, k, yo, ssk, k4.

Row 4: Sl, k2, ssk, yo, k3, yo, sl1, k2tog, psso, yo, k3, yo, k2tog, p3.

Rows 5–8: Repeat rows 1–4.

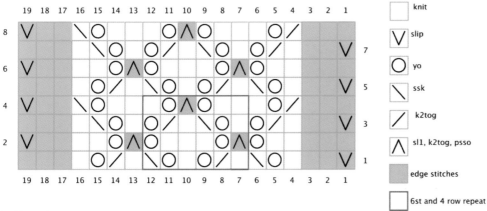

Bead Lace chart.

Horseshoe Lace

This is another traditional and very familiar lace which is identical to the Estonian Peacock Tail motif. In fact, this lace motif appears in many lace traditions with a variety of names. In this version, in keeping with the Shetland tradition, it is worked in garter stitch and therefore has no right or wrong side. The wrong side rows, however, can be purled, as is more commonly seen in the Estonian version.

Horseshoe Lace Instructions

Row 1: Sl, k2, yo, k3, sl1, k2tog, psso, k3, yo, k, yo, k3, sl1, k2tog, psso, k3, yo, k3. (25 sts)

Row 2: Sl, k24.

Row 3: Sl, (k3, yo, k2, sl1, k2tog, psso, k2, yo) × 2, k4.

Row 4: Sl, k24.

Row 5: Sl, k4, (yo, k, sl1, k2tog, psso, k, yo, k5) × 2.

Row 6: Sl, k24.

Row 7: Sl, k5, yo, sl1, k2tog, psso, yo, k7, yo, sl1, k2tog, psso, yo, k6.

Row 8: Sl, k24.

Rows 9–16: Repeat rows 1–8.

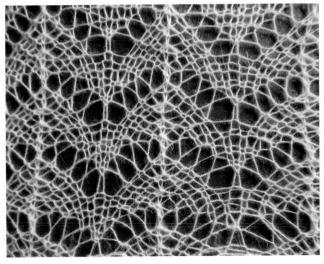

Horseshoe Lace.

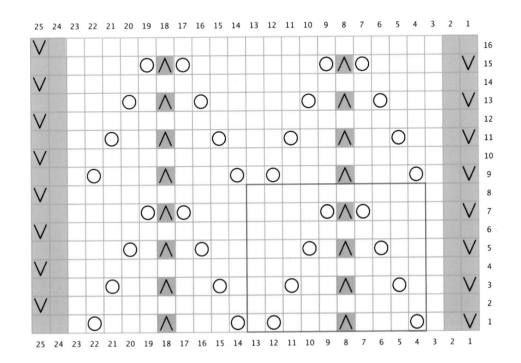

Horseshoe Lace chart.

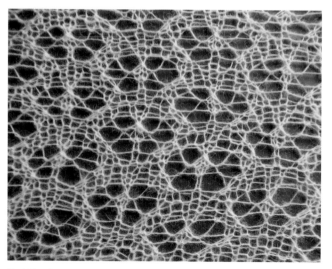

Cat's Paw Lace.

Cat's Paw Lace

This is the Shetland rendition of Cat's Paw. Paws turn up all over the place. However, whilst many are very similar to this pattern, this motif bears a particularly striking resemblance to an actual cat's paw print. This is knitted in garter stitch.

Cat's Paw Lace Instructions

Row 1: Sl, k2, (k2tog, yo, k, yo, ssk, k5) × 2, k2tog, yo, k, yo, ssk, k3. (31 sts)

Row 2: Sl, k30.

Row 3: Sl, k, (k2tog, yo, k3, yo, ssk, k3) × 2, k2tog, yo, k3, yo, ssk, k2.

Row 4: Sl, k30.

Row 5: Sl, k3, (yo, sl1, k2tog, psso, yo, k7) × 2, yo, sl1, k2tog, psso, yo, k4.

Row 6: Sl, k30.

Row 7: Sl, k7, k2tog, yo, k, yo, ssk, k5, k2tog, yo, k, yo, ssk, k8.

Row 8: Sl, k30.

Row 9: Sl, k, (yo, ssk, k3, k2tog, yo, k3) × 2, yo, ssk, k3, k2tog, yo, k2.

Row 10: Sl, k30.

Row 11: Sl, k8, yo, sl1, k2tog, psso, yo, k7, yo, sl1, k2tog, psso, yo, k9.

Row 12: Sl, k30.

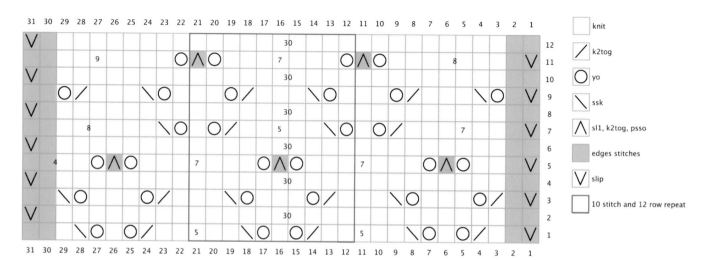

Cat's Paw Lace chart.

Mrs Hunter's Pattern

Mrs Hunter was a member of a well-known knitting family from Unst in the Shetland Isles, and is said to have been responsible for inventing this particular pattern. It is a lace pattern that uses a slip stitch to wrap three stitches at a time. It is equally attractive knitted in either garter stitch or stocking stitch. It is frequently used for baby blankets.

For this version knit all wrong side rows, slipping the first stitch, otherwise follow the chart.

Mrs Hunter's Pattern Instructions
Row 1 (RS): Sl, k15. (16 sts)
Row 2 (WS): Sl wyif, p15.
Row 3: Sl, k2, (sl, k3, psso) × 2, sl, ssk, k3.
Row 4: Sl wyif, (p3, yo) × 3, p3.

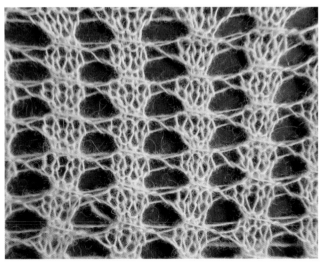

Garter stitch version.

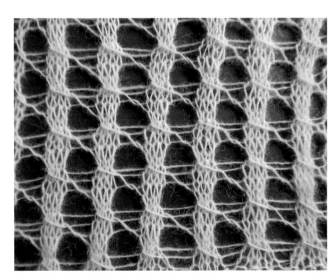

Stocking stitch version.

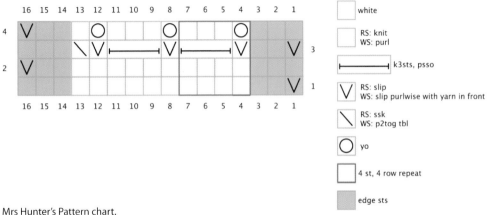

Mrs Hunter's Pattern chart.

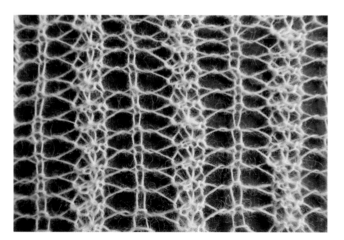

Razor Shell Lace, garter stitch version.

Razor Shell Lace

This is another attractive but simple design associated with the Shetland tradition. This is knitted in garter stitch but the even rows can be purled if wished.

Razor Shell Lace Instructions
Row 1 and all odd-numbered rows: Sl, k2, yo, k, sl1, k2tog, psso, (k, yo) × 2, k, sl1, k2tog, psso, k, yo, k3.
Row 2: Sl, k16 (17 sts).
Row 4: Sl, k16.
Row 6: Sl, k16.
Row 8: Sl, k16.

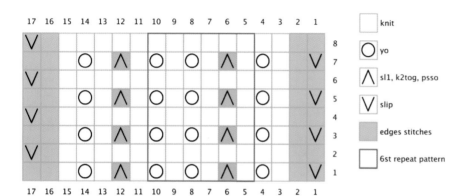

	knit
◯	yo
∧	sl1, k2tog, psso
V	slip
▨	edges stitches
☐	6st repeat pattern

Razor Shell Lace chart.

Mrs Montague's Pattern

This is another old pattern thought to date back to the days of Queen Elizabeth I. Mrs Montague's Pattern is an attractive motif and is not complicated to knit. This sample is created on a garter stitch ground, however, as with many of these old patterns, it can be found as a design on a stocking stitch ground very frequently in both knitting books and most online searches. It is a matter of personal preference as to which approach is chosen and it is not at all difficult to substitute a purl row for the knit row on my chart

Mrs Montague's Pattern Instructions
Multiples of 16 stitches + 9.

Row 1: Sl, k3, yo, ssk, k3, k2tog, yo, k9, yo, ssk, k3, k2tog, yo, k4. (31 sts).

Row 2: and all even numbered rows; Sl, k30.

Row 3: Sl, k4, yo, ssk, k, k2tog, yo, k3, k2tog, yo, k, yo, ssk, k3, yo, ssk, k, k2tog, yo, k5.

Row 5: Sl, k5, yo, sl1, k2tog, psso, yo, k3, k2tog, yo, k3, yo, ssk, k3, yo, sl1, k2tog, psso, yo, k6.

Row 7: Sl, k10, k2tog, yo, k5, yo, ssk, k11.

Row 9: Sl, k11, yo, ssk, k3, k2tog, yo, k12.

Row 11: Sl, k4, k2tog, yo, k, yo, ssk, k3, yo, ssk, k, k2tog, yo, k3, k2tog, yo, k, yo, ssk, k5.

Row 13: Sl, k3, k2tog, yo, k3, yo, ssk, k3, yo, sl1, k2tog, psso, yo, k3, k2tog, yo, k3, yo, ssk, k4.

Row 15: Sl, k2, k2tog, yo, k5, yo, ssk, k7, k2tog, yo, k5, yo, ssk, k3.

Row 17: Repeat row 1.

Row 19: Sl, k4, yo, ssk, k, k2tog, yo, k11, yo, ssk, k, k2tog, yo, k5.

Row 21: Sl, k5, yo, sl1, k2tog, psso, yo, k13, yo, sl1, k2tog, psso, yo, k6.

Row 22: Sl, k30.

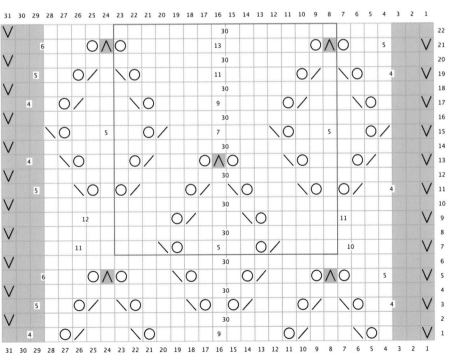

Mrs Montague's chart.

Mrs Montague's pattern.

Chart legend:
- ☐ knit
- Edge stitches
- O yo
- \ ssk
- / k2tog
- ∧ sl1, k2tog, psso
- Highlight for multiple dec
- ☐ 16 st, 16 row repeat
- V slip

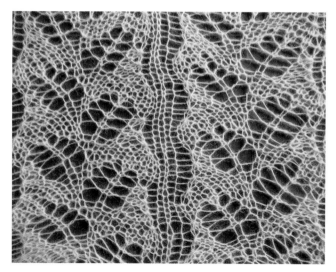

Fern Lace.

Fern Lace

This is another lace associated with the Shetland tradition, although similar motifs can be found in other traditions with different names. A very attractive motif which looks more complicated to make than it actually is. It can be used both as an edge stitch as well as an all over motif.

Fern Lace Instructions
Row 1: Sl, k2, (p2, k9, yo, k, yo, k3, sl1, k2tog, psso) × 2, p2, k3. (44 sts).

Row 2 and all even numbered rows Sl, k43.

Row 3: Sl, k2, (p2, k10, yo, k, yo, k2, sl1, k2tog, psso) × 2, p2, k3.

Row 5: Sl, k2, (p2, sl1, k2tog, psso, k4, yo, k, yo, k3, (yo, k) × 2, sl1, k2tog, psso) × 2, p2, k3.

Row 7: Sl, k2, (p2, sl1, k2tog, psso, k3, yo, k, yo, k9) × 2, p2, k3.

Row 9: Sl, k2, (p2, sl1, k2tog, psso, k2, yo, k, yo, k10) × 2, p2, k3.

Row 11: Sl, k2, (p2, sl1, k2tog, psso, (k, yo) × 2, k3, yo, k, yo, k4, sl1, k2tog, psso) × 2, p2, k3.

Row 12: Sl, k43.

☐	knit
•	purl
O	yo
∧	sl1, k2tog, psso
☐	18 st and 12 row repeat
▨	edge stitches
V	slip

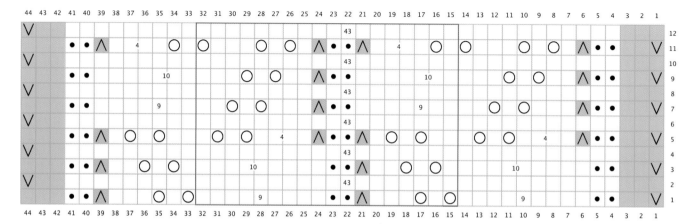

Fern Lace chart.

Fir Cone Lace

This lovely old pattern is simple to knit. It forms pouches during knitting due to the nature of the decreases, which pull out when it is stretched to reveal a pattern that does indeed look a lot like a pine cone. It is knitted on a garter background.

Fir Cone Lace Instructions
Multiples of 10 stitches + 11 side stitches

Row 1: K3, yo, k3, sl1, k2tog, psso, k3, yo, k, yo, k3, sl1, k2tog, psso, k3, yo, k3. (25 sts).
Row 2 and all even-numbered rows: Knit.
Row 3: Repeat row 1.
Row 5: Repeat row 1.
Row 7: Repeat row 1.
Row 9: K2, k2tog, k3, yo, k, yo, k3, sl1, k2tog, psso, k3, yo, k, yo, k3, ssk, k2.
Row 11: Repeat row 9.
Row 13: Repeat row 9.

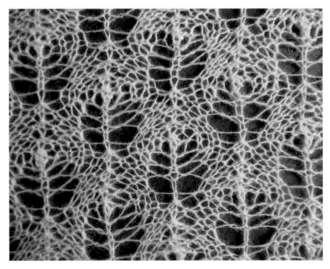

Fir Cone Lace.

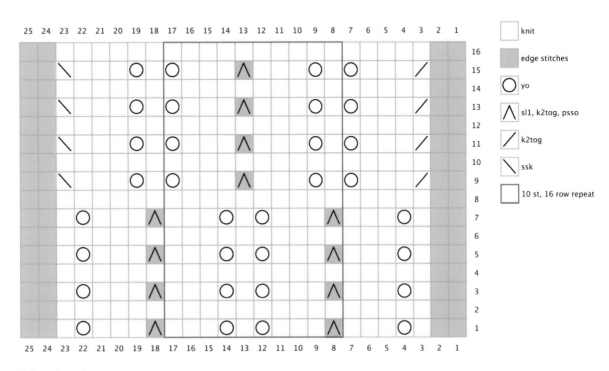

Fir Cone Lace chart.

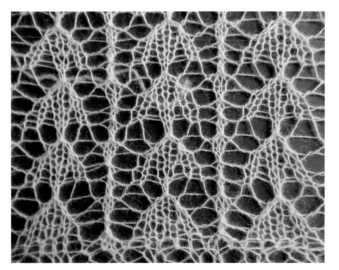

Harebell Lace.

Harebell or Snowdrop Lace

This pattern requires purl stitches, but the lace is only patterned on the right-side rows, so this is a straightforward knit with very pretty results. The pattern does have a right and wrong way up so for scarves or stoles it will need to be grafted in the middle so that the pattern balances.

Harebell Lace Instructions

Row 1 (RS): Sl, k2, ssk, yo, k, yo, sl1, k2tog, psso, yo, k6, yo, k2tog, k3. (20 sts)

Row 2 and all WS rows: Sl wyif, k2, p14, k3.

Row 3: Repeat row 1.

Row 5: Sl, k2, ssk, yo, k4, yo, ssk, k, k2tog, yo, k, yo, k2tog, k3.

Row 7: Sl, k2, ssk, (yo, k, yo, sl1, k2tog, psso) × 2, yo, k2, yo, k2tog, k3.

Row 9: Repeat row 1.

Row 11: Repeat row 1.

Row 13: Repeat row 5.

Row 15: Repeat row 7.

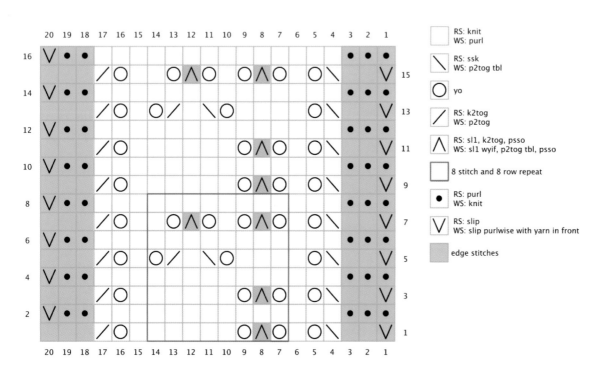

Harebell Lace chart.

Print of the Wave

This is a pattern that requires purl stitches to make it work. It is perhaps one of the most attractive patterns and also a very well-known motif which was often used in shawls by the Victorian lace knitters of the Shetland Islands. Again, similar motifs with different names are not uncommon in other lace traditions.

Print of the Wave Instructions
Multiples of 17 stitches + 10.

Row 1 (RS): Sl, k4, (k2tog, yo) × 3, k, yo, k2, ssk, k4, k2tog, k2, (yo, k2tog) × 2, yo, k5. (33 sts)

Row 2 and all WS rows: Sl wyif, p32.

Row 3: Sl, k3, (k2tog, yo) × 3, k3, yo, k2, ssk, k2, k2tog, k2, (yo, k2tog) × 2, yo, k6.

Row 5: Sl, k2, (k2tog, yo) × 3, k5, yo, k2, ssk, k2tog, k2, (yo, k2tog) × 2, yo, k7.

Row 7: Sl, k4, (yo, ssk) × 2, yo, k2, ssk, k4, k2tog, k2, yo, k, (yo, ssk) × 3, k5.

Row 9: Sl, k5, (yo, ssk) × 2, yo, k2, ssk, k2, k2tog, k2, yo, k3, (yo, ssk) × 3, k4.

Row 11: Sl, k6, (yo, ssk) × 2, yo, k2, ssk, k2tog, k2, yo, k5, (yo, ssk) × 3, k3.

Row 13: Repeat row 1.

Row 15: Repeat row 3.

Row 17: Repeat row 5.

Row 19: Repeat row 7.

Row 21: Repeat row 9.

Row 23: Repeat row 11.

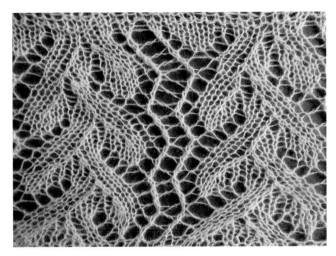

Print of the Wave.

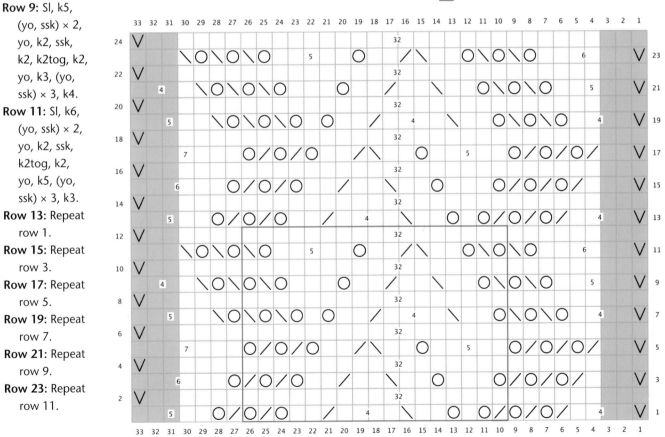

Print of the Wave chart.

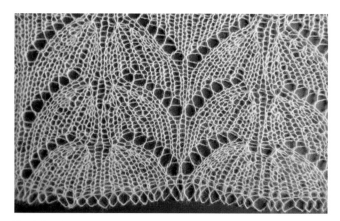

Bear's Paw Lace.

Bear's Paw or Umbrella Lace

This very attractive stitch can be used both as an edging stitch or as an all over pattern.

Bear's Paw Instructions
Multiples of 18 stitches +1.

Row 1 (RS): K, yo, (k, p3) × 4, k, yo, k. (21 sts)
Row 2 and all WS rows: Purl.
Row 3: K2, yo, (k, p3) × 4, k, yo, k2. (23 sts)
Row 5: K3, yo, (k, p3) × 4, k, yo, k3. (25 sts)
Row 7: K4, yo, (k, p2tog, p) × 4, k, yo, k4. (23 sts)
Row 9: K5, yo, (k, p2tog) × 4, k, yo, k5. (21 sts)
Row 11: K6, yo, (k, k3tog) × 2, k, yo, k6. (19 sts)

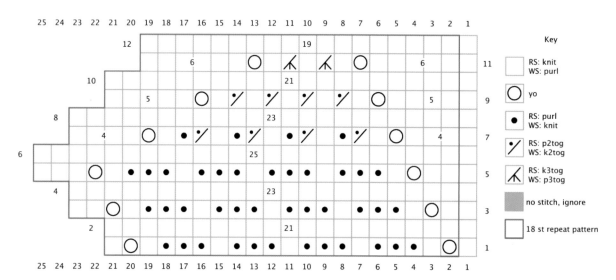

Bear's Paw Lace chart.

Frost Flowers, or Spanish Lace Stitch

This is another old pattern, and one that looks rather complicated. The chart may appear a little daunting if you are less familiar with working from charts, however, in reality, it is a relatively simple four-row pattern which is repeated three times. The pattern then does a half drop, which is also repeated three times. All in all, there are thirty-four stitches and twenty-four rows to each full pattern repeat. It is quite an easy pattern to learn after the first few pattern repeats. The chart includes three garter stitch border stitches on either side to provide a frame. This is a spectacular pattern and well worth the effort of knitting.

Frost Flowers Instructions
Multiples of 34 stitches + 2.

Row 1 (RS): Sl, k5, k2tog, k4, yo, p2, (k2, yo, ssk) × 3, p2, yo, k4, ssk, k6. (40 sts)

Row 2 (WS): Sl wyif, k2, p2, p2tog tbl, p4, yo, p, k2, (p2, yo, p2tog) × 3, k2, p, yo, p4, p2tog, p2, k3.

Row 3: Sl, k3, k2tog, k4, yo, k2, p2, (k2, yo, ssk) × 3, p2, k2, yo, k4, ssk, k4.

Row 4: Sl wyif, k2, p2tog tbl, p4, yo, p3, k2, (p2, yo, p2tog) × 3, k2, p3, yo, p4, p2tog, k3.

Rows 5–12: Repeat rows 1–4.

Row 13: Sl, (k2, yo, ssk) × 2, p2, yo, k4, ssk, k6, k2tog, k4, yo, p2, k2, yo, ssk, k5.

Row 14: Sl wyif, k2, yo, p2tog, p2, yo, p2tog, k2, p, yo, p4, p2tog, p4, p2tog tbl, p4, yo, p, k2, p2, yo, p2tog, p2, k3.

Row 15: Sl, (k2, yo, ssk) × 2, p2, k2, yo, k4, ssk, k2, k2tog, k4, yo, k2, p2, k2, yo, ssk, k5.

Row 16: Sl wyif, k2, yo, p2tog, p2, yo, p2tog, k2, p3, yo, p4, p2tog, p2tog tbl, p4, yo, p3, k2, p2, yo, p2tog, p2, k3.

Rows 17–24: Repeat rows 13–16.

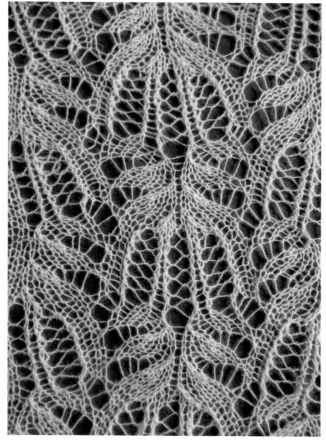

Frost Flowers.

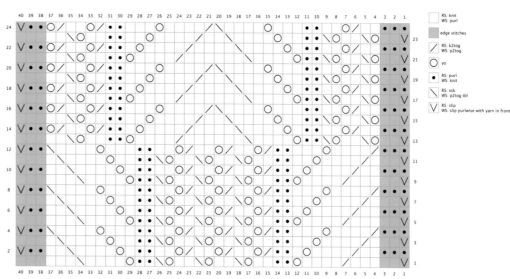

Frost Flowers chart.

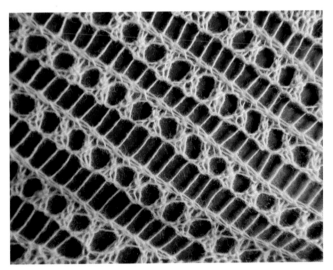

Spanish Diagonal Lace.

Spanish Diagonal Lace

Yet another old lace said to be from Spain. This is a straight-forward diagonal lace pattern that is very effective, but it is not so commonly seen in current lace knitting. It produces a beautiful airy and slightly textured lace although the effects with heavier weight yarns can be just as interesting.

Spanish Diagonal Lace Instructions

Row 1: Sl, k4, (yo, ssk, k, k2tog, yo, k3) × 2, yo, ssk, k, k2tog, yo, k8. (34 sts)

Row 2: Sl, k9, (p2tog, yo, k6) × 3.

Row 3: Sl, k6, (yo, ssk, k, k2tog, yo, k3) × 2, yo, ssk, k, k2tog, yo, k6.

Row 4: Sl, k7,(p2tog,yo, k6,) x2 p2tog yo, k8.

Row 5: Sl, k8, (yo, ssk, k, k2tog, yo, k3) × 2, yo, ssk, k7.

Row 6: Sl, k5, (p2tog, yo, k6) × 3, k4.

Row 7: Sl, k5, (k2tog, yo, k3, yo, ssk, k) × 2, k2tog, yo, k3, yo, ssk, k5.

Row 8: Sl, k3 (p2tog,yo, k6) × 3, p2tog, yo, k4.

Rows 9–16: Repeat rows 1–8.

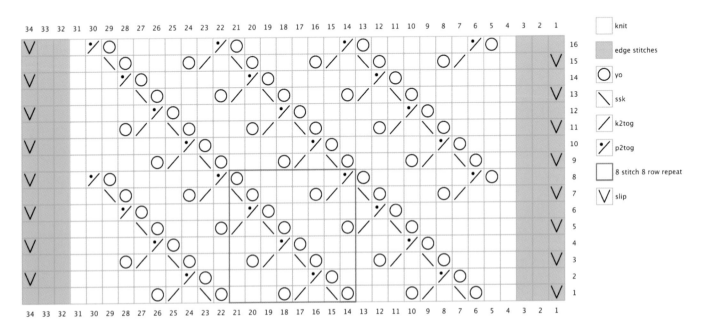

Spanish Diagonal Lace chart.

Old Shell, or Old Shale

This is another traditional pattern very closely associated with the Shetland Isles. For some reason and at some point in the past, it became confused with the Feather and Fan motif. Subsequently this confusion became widespread, and now the two stitch patterns are invariably misnamed in both books, and in any search of the internet. A brief comparison shows that the two patterns are constructed a little differently. Old Shell has decreases which are spread over six stitches on either side of the yarn over increases and which are knitted as knit 2 together, which on a pattern repeat results in decreases over twelve stitches, alternated with the yarn over increases. For a comparison with Feather and Fan, please see the details regarding that motif.

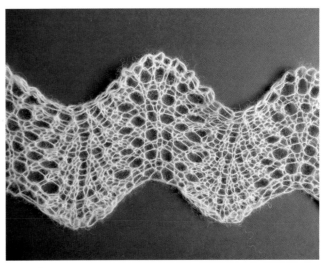

Old Shell.

Old Shell Instructions

This is the garter stitch version. For the purl version row 2 is purled.

Multiples of 18 stitches + 6 edge stitches.

Row 1 (RS): Sl, k41. (42 sts)
Row 2 (WS): Knit.
Row 3: Sl, k2, k2tog × 3, (yo, k) × 6, k2tog × 6, (yo, k) × 6, k2tog × 3, k3.
Row 4: Sl, k41.
Repeat these 4 rows.

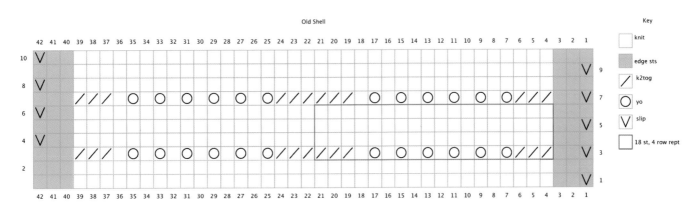

Old Shell chart.

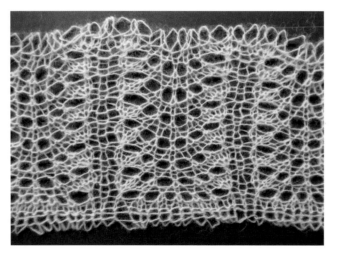

Feather and Fan.

Feather and Fan

By way of the comparison with Old Shell with which this motif is frequently confused, you can see that with Feather and Fan the decreases are grouped as knit 4 together on either side of the yarn over increases, which on a pattern repeat results in two mass decreases separated by one stitch followed by the six yarn over increases. This results in a much narrower channel of decreased stitches between the increases than is seen in Old Shell. This is therefore a different pattern, albeit using similar techniques to Old Shell, equally as attractive but not the same.

Feather and Fan Instructions

Multiples of 14 stitches + 1.

Row 1: Sl, (k, k4tog, (yo, k) × 5, yo, k4tog) × 2, k2. (31 sts)
Row 2: Sl, k30.
Row 3: Sl, k30.
Row 4: sl, k30.
Rows 5–8: Repeat Rows 1–4.

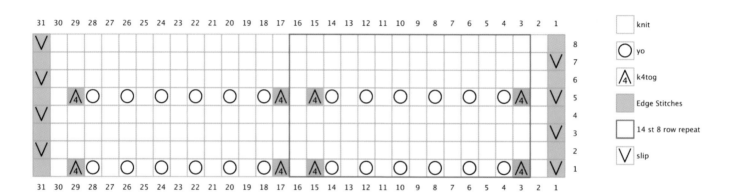

Feather and Fan chart.

Twist Cable and Lace

This is an attractive pattern that works equally well in both fine and heavier weight yarns. Whilst the cable twist may seem a little fiddly to begin with it becomes easier with repetition and is worth the perseverance. Whilst this can be used as an all over lace pattern it could equally well be placed as a panel or insertion along the side of a wrap or the centre of a cushion cover, for example.

Twist Cable and Lace Instructions

Row 1 (RS): Sl, (k3, k2tog, yo × 2, ssk) × 3, k4. (26 sts)

Row 2 (WS): Sl wyif, p4, (k tbl, k, p5) × 3.

Row 3: Sl, k3, (k2tog, yo × 2, ssk, cable twist 3) × 2, k2tog, yo × 2, ssk, k4.

Rows 4–5: Repeat rows 2–3.

Row 6: Repeat row 2.

Row 7: Repeat row 3.

Row 8: Repeat row 2.

Special Instruction

Cable Twist 3:

Knit into third st on the left-hand needle, then second st, then first st, and finally slip all three stitches onto the right-hand needle.

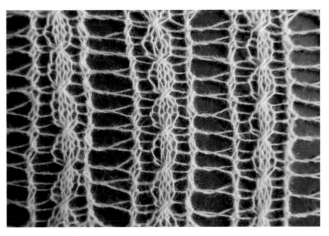

Twist Cable and Lace chart.

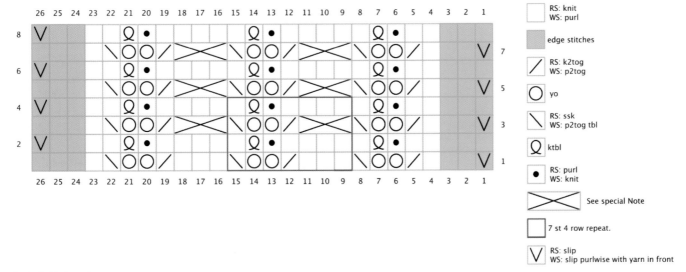

Twist Cable lace chart.

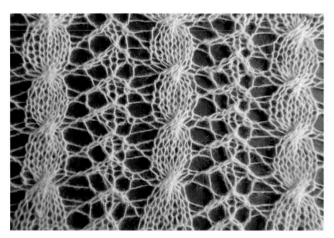

Lace and Cable.

Lace and Cable, or Germaine Stitch

This is a very dainty combination of lace and cables and is not difficult to knit. It looks equally good in heavier weight yarns and is an ideal stitch for sweaters and cardigans, or even socks. Whilst it is an all over pattern, it would work equally well used as a panel or insertion in garments, cushion covers or throws.

Lace and Cable Instructions
Multiples of 11 stitches + 7.

Row 1 (RS): Sl, k3, (yo, k2tog, k, ssk, yo, k6) × 2, yo, k2tog, k, ssk, yo, k4. (35 sts)
Row 2 and all WS rows: Sl wyif, p34.
Row 3: Sl, k4, (yo, sl1, k2tog, psso, yo, k, 3/3 RC, k) × 2, yo, sl1, k2tog, psso, yo, k5.
Row 5: Repeat row 1.
Row 7: Repeat row 3.
Row 9: Repeat row 1.
Row 11: Repeat row 3.

Special Instruction
3/3 RC. Slip three stitches onto the cable needle and hold at the back.
　Knit next three stitches, then knit three from the cable needle.

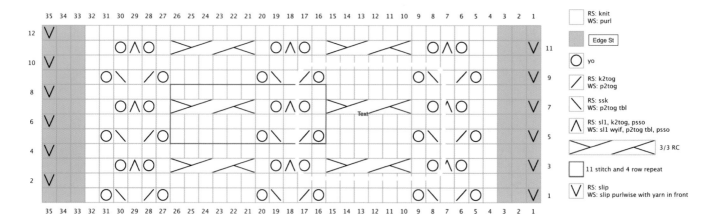

Lace and Cable chart.

Crest of the Wave

This is another old pattern associated with the Shetland Lace tradition. This swatch is knitted on a garter ground; however, it also works well if the even rows are purled and then rows 11 to 14 are in garter stitch. You could vary it further by knitting rows 11 to 14 in an alternative colour if you wished.

Crest of the Wave Instructions
Multiples of 12 stitches + 13.

Row 1 (RS): Sl, k3, (yo, k, yo, ssk × 2, k, k2tog × 2, (yo, k) × 2) × 2, yo, k, yo, ssk × 2, k, k2tog × 2, yo, k, yo, k4. (43 sts)
Row 2 and all WS rows: Sl, k42.
Row 3: Repeat row 1.
Row 5: Repeat row 1.
Row 7: Repeat row 1.
Row 9: Repeat row 1.
Row 11: Sl, k42.
Row 13: Sl, k42.

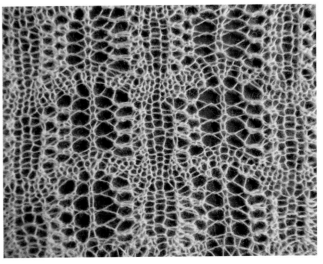

Crest of the Wave.

	(blank)	knit
	V	slip
	O	yo
	\	ssk
	/	k2tog
	(box)	12 st 14 row repeat

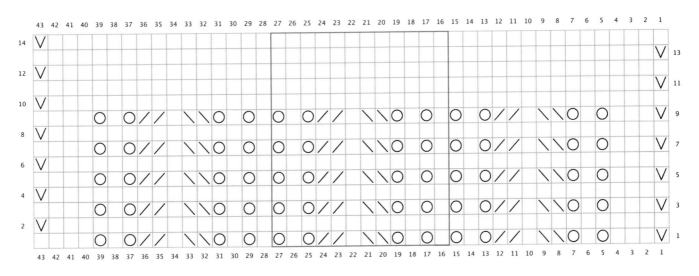

Row	43	42	41	40	39	38	37	36	35	34	33	32	31	30	29	28	27	26	25	24	23	22	21	20	19	18	17	16	15	14	13	12	11	10	9	8	7	6	5	4	3	2	1	Row
14	V																																											
																																											V	13
12	V																																											
																																											V	11
10	V																																											
					O		O	/	/		\	\	O		O		O		O	/	/		\	\	O		O		O		O	/	/		\	\	O		O				V	9
8	V																																											
					O		O	/	/		\	\	O		O		O		O	/	/		\	\	O		O		O		O	/	/		\	\	O		O				V	7
6	V																																											
					O		O	/	/		\	\	O		O		O		O	/	/		\	\	O		O		O		O	/	/		\	\	O		O				V	5
4	V																																											
					O		O	/	/		\	\	O		O		O		O	/	/		\	\	O		O		O		O	/	/		\	\	O		O				V	3
2	V																																											
					O		O	/	/		\	\	O		O		O		O	/	/		\	\	O		O		O		O	/	/		\	\	O		O				V	1

Crest of the Wave chart.

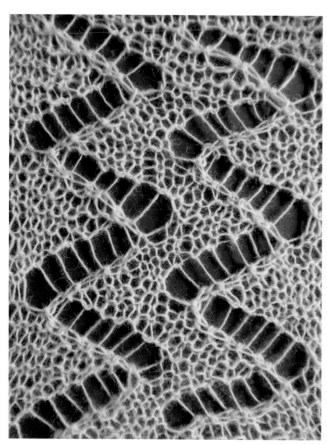

Zigzag Lace.

Vandyke, or Zigzag Lace

This is a lovely motif, easily knitted with the stitches moving back and forth one at a time to create the zigzag. It produces a motif that is full of movement. It could be used as an all over lace if wished, and can be easily paired with its mirror image to create balance. It is simply constructed and an easy knit.

Vandyke Zigzag Lace Instructions
Multiples of 8 stitches.

Row 1: Sl, k7, k2tog, yo, k6, k2tog, yo, k2. (20 sts)
Row 2: Sl, k3, yo, k2tog, k6, yo, k2tog, k7.
Row 3: Sl, k5, k2tog, yo, k6, k2tog, yo, k4.
Row 4: Sl, k4, yo, k2tog k6 yo, k2tog, k5.
Row 5: Sl, k3, (k2tog, yo, k6) × 2.
Row 6: Sl, k6, yo, k2tog, k6yo, k2tog, k3.
Row 7: Sl, k6, k2tog, yo, k6, k2tog, yo, k8.
Row 8: Sl, k7, ssk yo, k6, ssk yo, k2.
Row 9: Sl, k2, yo, ssk, k6, yo, ssk, k7.
Row 10: Sl, k5, ssk yo, k6, ssk yo, k4.
Row 11: Sl, k4, yo, ssk, k6, yo, ssk, k5.
Row 12: Sl, k3, ssk yo, k6, ssk, yo, k6.
Row 13: Sl, (k6, yo, ssk) × 2, k3.
Row 14: Sl,k1, ssk yo, k6, ssk, yo, k8.

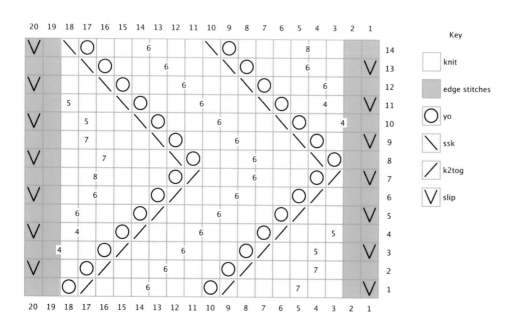

Zigzag Lace chart.

Lace Diamond

A very pretty pattern of a small diamond on a garter stitch background. This makes a lovely all over pattern and is not too challenging to complete. This sample is worked on a garter stitch ground but the pattern can also be worked on a stocking stitch ground. Experiment and see which you prefer.

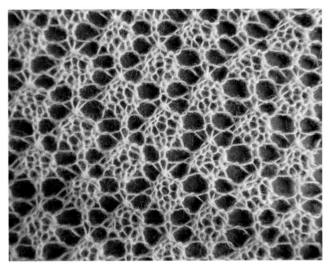

Lace Diamond.

Lace Diamond Instructions
Multiples of 6 stitches + 1.

Row 1: Sl, k3, (k2tog, yo, k, yo, ssk, k) × 2, k2tog, yo, k, yo, ssk, k4. (25 sts)

Row 2: Sl, k24.

Row 3: Sl, k2, k2tog, (yo, k3, yo, sl1, k2tog, psso) × 2, yo, k3, yo, ssk, k3.

Row 4: Sl, k24.

Row 5: Sl, k3, (yo, ssk, k, k2tog, yo, k) × 2, yo, ssk, k, k2tog, yo, k4.

Row 6: Sl, k24.

Row 7: Sl, k4, (yo, sl1, k2tog, psso, yo, k3) × 2, yo, sl1, k2tog, psso, yo, k5.

Row 8: Sl, k24.

Rows 9–16: Repeat Rows 1–8.

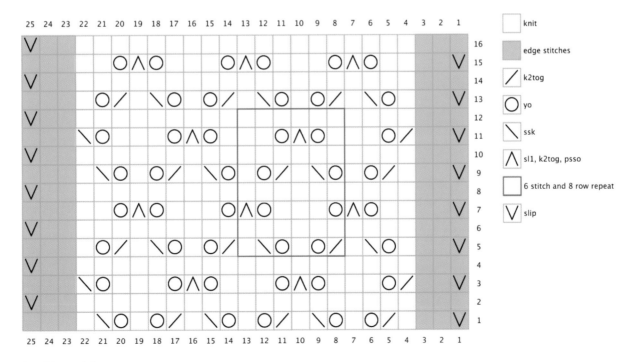

Lace Diamond chart.

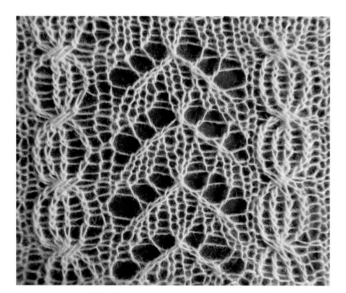
Chevron Lace and Cable.

Chevron Lace and Cable

This attractive lacy cable pattern works as either an all over design or as a panel, and looks equally good in both fine and thicker yarns.

Chevron Lace and Cable Instructions
Multiples of 21 stitches.

Row 1 (RS): P2, k tbl × 4, p1, yo, k2tog tbl, k3, k2tog, yo, p1, k tbl × 4, p2. (21 sts)
Row 2 and all WS rows: P2, p tbl × 4, k1, p7, k1, p tbl × 4, p2.
Row 3: P2, k tbl × 4, p1, k1, yo, k2tog tbl, k1, k2tog, yo, k1, p1, k tbl × 4, p2.
Row 5: P2, 2/2 RC, p1, k2, yo, sl1, k2tog, psso, yo, k2, p1, 2/2 LC, p2.
Row 7: P2, k tbl × 4, p1, k7, p1, k tbl × 4, p2.

Special Instructions
2/2 LC: Slip next 2 stitches to cable needle and place at front of work, k2, then k2 from cable needle.

2/2 RC: Slip next 2 stitches to cable needle and place at back of work, k2, then k2 from cable needle.

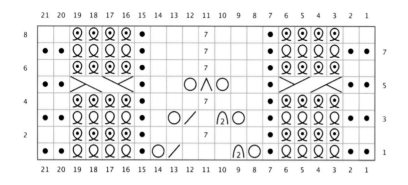

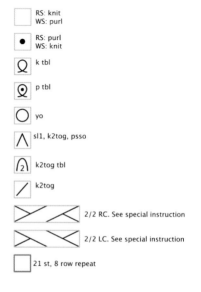

Chevron Lace and Cable chart.

Falling Leaves

This pretty pattern is a useful all over motif and is equally appealing in both garter and stocking stitch. This sample is worked with the wrong side rows in purl which really shows the leaves to good advantage, but means that there is an obvious wrong and right side.

Falling Leaves Instructions
Multiples of 10 stitches + 6.

Row 1 (RS): Sl, k3, (yo, k3, sl1, k2tog, psso, k3, yo, k) × 2, yo, k3, ssk, k3. (32 sts)

Row 2 and all WS rows: Sl wyif, p31.

Row 3: Sl, k4, (yo, k2, sl1, k2tog, psso, k2, yo, k3) × 2, yo, k2, ssk, k3.

Row 5: Sl, (k5, yo, k, sl1, k2tog, psso, k, yo) × 2, k5, yo, k, ssk, k3.

Row 7: Sl, k6, (yo, sl1, k2tog, psso, yo, k7) × 2, yo, ssk, k3.

Row 9: Sl, k2, k2tog, (k3, yo, k, yo, k3, sl1, k2tog, psso) × 2, k3, yo, k4.

Row 11: Sl, k2, k2tog, (k2, yo, k3, yo, k2, sl1, k2tog, psso) × 2, k2, yo, k5.

Row 13: Sl, k2, k2tog, (k, yo, k5, yo, k, sl1, k2tog, psso) × 2, k, yo, k6.

Row 15: Sl, k2, k2tog, (yo, k7, yo, sl1, k2tog, psso) × 2, yo, k7.

Repeat these rows.

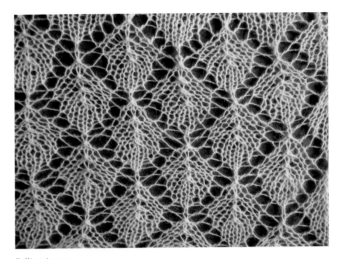

Falling Leaves.

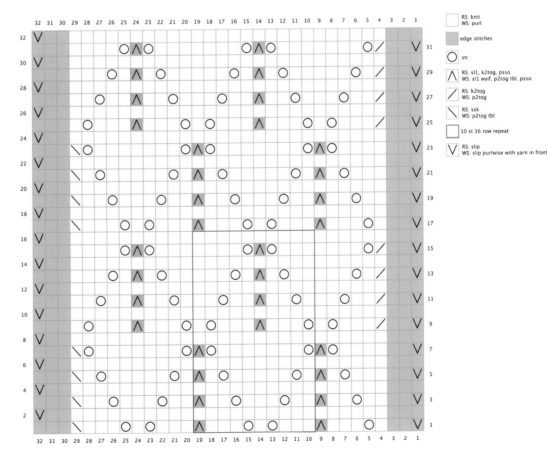

Falling Leaves chart.

☐	RS: knit WS: purl
▨	edge stitches
O	yo
Λ	RS: sl1, k2tog, psso WS: sl1 wyif, p2tog tbl, psso
╱	RS: k2tog WS: p2tog
╲	RS: ssk WS: p2tog tbl
☐	10 st 16 row repeat
V	RS: slip WS: slip purlwise with yarn in front

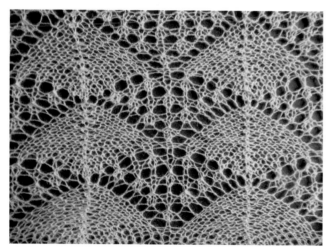

Madeira Cascade.

Madeira Cascade

This is one of a number of patterns described as Madeira lace. As a group, they are generally ascribed as being probably of Spanish origin. This is interesting as Madeira is a Portuguese island that, as far as I know, has never been owned or occupied by Spain so the naming of these patterns provides yet another mystery. This particular pattern is very pretty, and being knitted in garter stitch provides an excellent both sides pattern.

Madeira Cascade Instructions
Multiples of 20 stitches + 5.

Row 1: (Sl, k4, yo, k8, sl1, k2tog, psso, k8, yo, k, yo, k8, sl1, k2tog, psso, k8, yo, k4), k3. (51 sts)
Row 2: Sl, k50.
Row 3: (Sl, k5, yo, k7, sl1, k2tog, psso, k7, yo, k3, yo, k7, sl1, k2tog, psso, k7, yo, k5), k3.
Row 4: Sl, k50.
Row 5: (Sl, k3, k2tog, (yo, k, yo, k6, sl1, k2tog, psso, k6, yo, k, yo, sl1, k2tog, psso) × 2, yo, k2), k3.
Row 6: Sl, k50.
Row 7: (Sl, (k7, yo, k5, sl1, k2tog, psso, k5, yo) × 2, k7), k3.
Row 8: Sl, k50.
Row 9: (Sl, k4, (yo, sl1, k2tog, psso, yo, k, yo, k4, sl1, k2tog, psso, k4, yo, k, yo, sl1, k2tog, psso, yo, k) × 2, yo, ssk, k), k3.
Row 10: Sl, k50.
Row 11: (Sl, k9, yo, k3, sl1, k2tog, psso, k3, yo, k11, yo, k3, sl1, k2tog, psso, k3, yo, k9), k3.
Row 12: Sl, k50.
Row 13: (Sl, k3, k2tog, (yo, k, yo, sl1, k2tog, psso, yo, k, yo, k2, sl1, k2tog, psso, k2, (yo, k, yo, sl1, k2tog, psso) × 2) × 2, yo, k2), k3.
Row 14: Sl, k50.
Row 15: (Sl, k11, yo, k, sl1, k2tog, psso, k, yo, k15, yo, k, sl1, k2tog, psso, k, yo, k11), k3.
Row 16: Sl, k50.
Row 17: (Sl, k4, (yo, sl1, k2tog, psso, yo, k) × 10, yo, ssk, k), k3.
Row 18: Sl, k50.
Rows 19–36: Repeat rows 1–18.

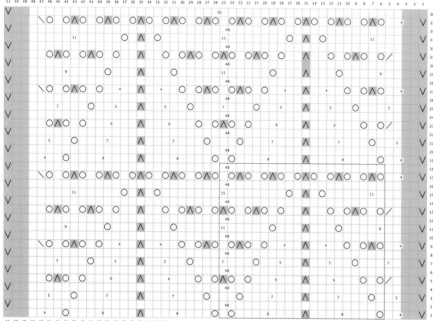

Madeira Cascade chart.

Panels and insertions

Panels and insertions are traditionally used in the construction of knitted shawls and provide frames and divisions between all over lace patterns and the edgings. As well their use as above, it is easy to see that these designs can also be used to add interest to knitted garments, for example, a panel down the front of a cardigan, or in the centre of a cushion cover, or around the bottom of a sweater or around a neckline or cuff, between the main knitting and the welt.

Leaf Panel

This motif is knitted here on a garter stitch ground, but would look well in thicker yarns on a stocking stitch ground. Again, this is not a difficult pattern and is an extremely attractive and versatile motif.

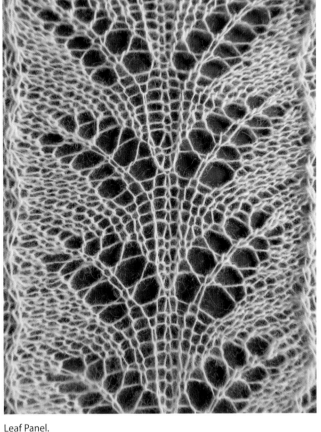

Leaf Panel.

Leaf Panel Instructions

Row 1 (RS): Sl, k, sl1, k2tog, psso, k7, yo, k, yo, p2, yo, k, yo, k7, k3tog, k2. (28 sts)

Row 2 and all WS rows: Sl wyif, p27.

Row 3: Sl, k, sl1, k2tog, psso, k6, (yo, k) × 2, p2, (k, yo) × 2, k6, k3tog, k2.

Row 5: Sl, k, sl1, k2tog, psso, k5, yo, k, yo, k2, p2, k2, yo, k, yo, k5, k3tog, k2.

Row 7: Sl, k, sl1, k2tog, psso, k4, yo, k, yo, k3, p2, k3, yo, k, yo, k4, k3tog, k2.

Row 9: Sl, k, sl1, k2tog, psso, k3, yo, k, yo, k4, p2, k4, yo, k, yo, k3, k3tog, k2.

Row 11: Repeat row 1.

Row 13: Repeat row 3.

Row 15: Repeat row 5.

Row 17: Repeat row 7.

Row 19: Repeat row 9.

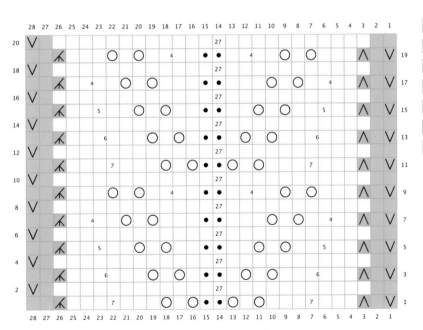

Leaf Panel chart.

Legend:

(empty box)	RS: knit / WS: purl
O	yo
•	RS: purl / WS: knit
∧	RS: sl1, k2tog, psso / WS: sl1 wyif, p2tog tbl, psso
⅄	RS: k3tog / WS: p3tog
(grey box)	edge stitches
V	RS: slip / WS: slip purlwise with yarn in front

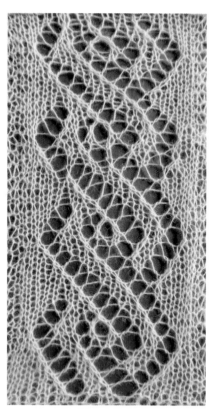

Lace Diamond Chain.

Lace Diamond Chain

A beautiful, classic panel motif, graceful and elegant. It was worked on a stocking stitch ground, which looks good in whatever weight of yarn is used and is a lovely panel to team with a cable perhaps for an attractive winter sweater.

Lace Diamond Chain Instructions
Row 1 (RS): Sl, k5, yo, ssk, k2, yo, ssk, k6. (18 sts)
Row 2 and all WS rows: Sl wyif, p17.
Row 3: Sl, k3, k2tog, yo, k, yo, ssk, k2, yo, ssk, k5.
Row 5: Sl, k2, k2tog, yo, k3, yo, ssk, k2, yo, ssk, k4.
Row 7: Sl, k, k2tog, yo, k2, k2tog, yo, k, yo, ssk, k2, yo, ssk, k3.
Row 9: Sl, k2tog, yo, k2, k2tog, yo, k3, (yo, ssk, k2) × 2.
Row 11: Sl, (k2, yo, ssk) × 2, yo, k2tog, yo, k2, k2tog, yo, k2tog, k.
Row 13: Sl, k3, yo, ssk, k2, yo, sl1, k2tog, psso, yo, k2, k2tog, yo, k3.
Row 15: Sl, k4, yo, ssk, k2, yo, ssk, k, k2tog, yo, k4.

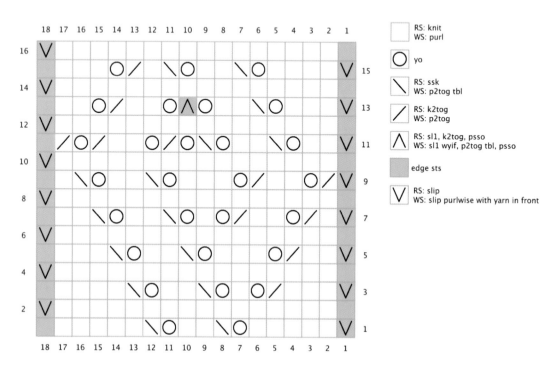

Lace Diamond Chain chart.

Ladder Insertion

A useful pattern for creating frames and dividing between different lace motifs. You can use this as a single column or add additional lines of ladders separated by single or multiple stitches.

Ladder Lace Insertion Instructions
Row 1 and all RS rows: K3, yo, ssk, k.
Row 2 and all WS rows: K3, yo, K2tog, K.

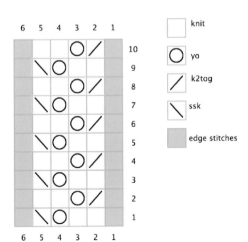

Ladder Insertion chart.

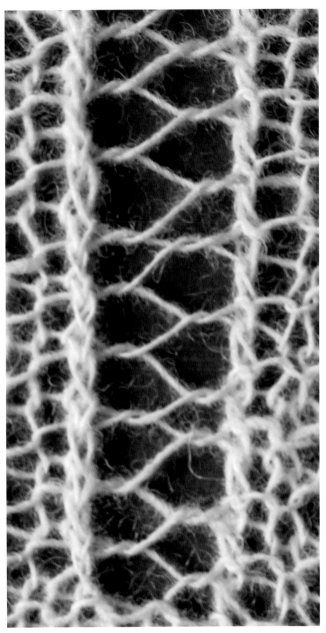

Ladder Insertion

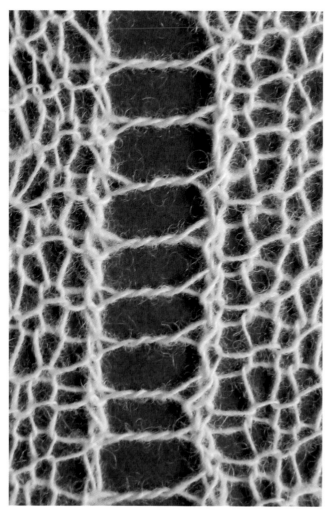

Lace Holes.

Lace Holes Insertion

Another useful dividing and framing pattern.

Lace Holes Insertion Instructions
Row 1 (RS): K4, k2tog, yo × 2, ssk, k4. (12 sts)
Row 2 (WS): K6, p, k5.
Row 3: K2, (k2tog, yo × 2, ssk) × 2, k2.
Row 4: K4, (p, k3) × 2.
Rows 5–12: Repeat rows 1–4.

Lace Holes chart.

		knit
	/	k2tog
	\	ssk
	•	purl
	O	yo
		edges stitches

Chevrons

Chevrons are a very familiar pattern, and frequently seen in cable and texture patterns. They are equally attractive in lace and work well both as border patterns and as all over patterns.

Chevron Lace Instructions

Row 1 (RS): K6, k2tog, k2, yo, p, yo, k2, ssk, k6. (21 sts)
Row 2 and all WS rows: Purl.
Row 3: K5, k2tog, k2, yo, k, p, k, yo, k2, ssk, k5.
Row 5: K4, k2tog, k2, yo, k2, p, k2, yo, k2, ssk, k4.
Row 7: K3, k2tog, k2, yo, k3, p, k3, yo, k2, ssk, k3.
Row 9: K2, k2tog, k2, yo, k4, p, k4, yo, k2, ssk, k2.
Row 11: Repeat row 1.
Row 13: Repeat row 3.
Row 15: Repeat row 5.
Row 17: Repeat row 7.
Row 19: Repeat row 9.

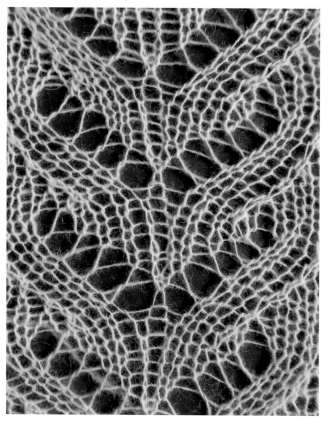

Chevron Lace.

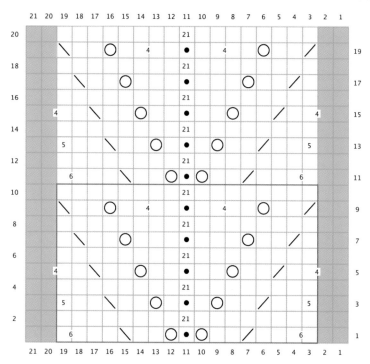

Chevron Lace chart.

	RS: knit WS: purl
	edge stitches
/	RS: k2tog WS: p2tog
O	yo
\	RS: ssk WS: p2tog tbl
•	RS: purl WS: knit
	17 st 10 row repeat

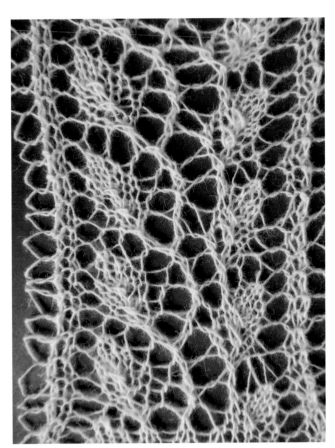

Double Rose Leaf insertion.

Double Rose Leaf Insertion

This graceful and elegant pattern is an old Victorian design.

Double Rose Leaf Insertion Instructions

Row 1 (RS): Yo, k2tog, k, yo, k5, yo, sl1, k2tog, psso, yo, ssk, sl1, k2tog, psso, (k, yo) × 2, k3. (21 sts)

Row 2 and all WS rows: Yo, k2tog, k, p15, k3.

Row 3: Yo, k2tog, k, yo, k2, sl1, k2tog, psso, k2, yo, ssk, yo, sl1, k2tog, psso, (yo, k3) × 2.

Row 5: Yo, k2tog, (k, yo) × 2, k, sl1, k2tog, psso, k, yo, sl1, k2tog, psso, yo, ssk, k4, yo, k3.

Row 7: Yo, k2tog, k, yo, k3, yo, sl1, k2tog, psso, yo, k2tog, yo, k2, sl1, k2tog, psso, k2, yo, k3.

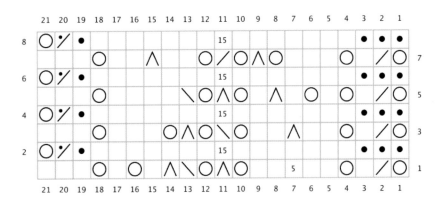

Double Rose Leaf insertion chart.

Zigzag Insertion

It is easy to increase the lines of zigzags by adding extra stitches. This insertion gives a lovely sense of movement, especially when added along the sides of a wrap or scarf.

Zigzag Insertion Instructions
Row 1 (RS): K2, (yo, ssk) × 2, k2. (8 sts)
Row 2 and all WS rows: Knit.
Row 3: K3, (yo, ssk) × 2, k.
Row 5: K4, (yo, ssk) × 2.
Row 7: K2, (k2tog, yo) × 2, k2.
Row 9: K, (k2tog, yo) × 2, k3.
Row 11: (K2tog, yo) × 2, k4.

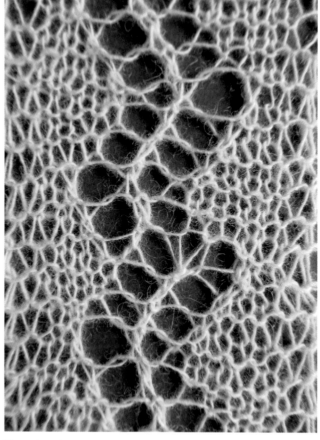

Zigzag insertion.

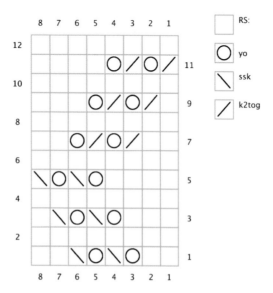

Zigzag insertion chart.

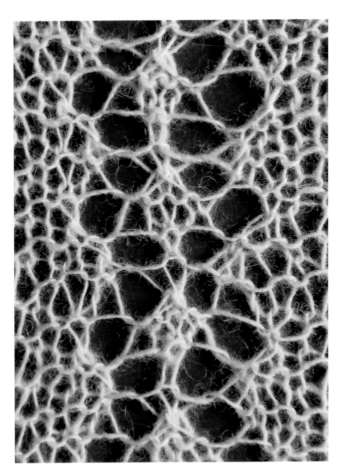

Cat's Paw insertion.

Cat's Paw Insertion

This insertion is the same motif as the all over lace pattern given earlier in this chapter. In this pattern, the motifs line up one above the other, creating a pretty panel of Cat's Paw.

Cat's Paw Insertion Instructions
Row 1 (RS): K3, k2tog, yo, k, yo, ssk, k3. (11 sts)
Row 2 and all WS rows: Purl.
Row 3: K2, k2tog, yo, k3, yo, ssk, k2.
Row 5: K4, yo, sl1, k2tog, psso, yo, k4.
Row 7: Repeat row 1.
Row 9: Repeat row 3.
Row 11: Repeat row 5.

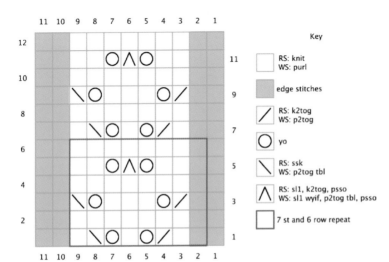

Cat's Paw insertion chart.

Day Flower, or Wheat Ear

This is an old pattern, probably Victorian, worked as a border. It is not as complex to knit as it looks and gives pleasing results.

Day Flower Border Instructions

Row 1 (RS): Sl, k, yo, k2tog, yo, k2tog × 3, k2, yo, k3, yo, k2tog, yo, k, yo × 2, k2. (22 sts)

Row 2 (WS): K3, p, k3, p13, k2.

Row 3: Sl, k, yo, k2tog, sl1, k2tog, psso × 2, yo, k, yo, k2, (k2tog, yo) × 2, k5. (20 sts)

Row 4: Bind off × 2, k4, p8, p2tog, p, k2. (17 sts)

Row 5: Sl, k, yo, sl1, k2tog, psso, yo, k3, yo, k2, (k2tog, yo) × 2, k, yo × 2, k2. (20 sts)

Row 6: K3, p, k3, p11, k2.

Row 7: Sl, k, yo, k2tog, yo, k, (yo, k2, k2tog) × 2, yo, k2tog, yo, k5. (22 sts)

Row 8: Bind off × 2, k4, p13, k2. (20 sts)

Row 9: Sl, k, yo, k2tog, yo, k3, yo, k2, k2tog, yo, ssk × 2, yo, k2tog, yo, k, yo × 2, k2. (23 sts)

Row 10: K3, p, k3, p14, k2.

Row 11: Sl, k, (yo, k2tog) × 2, k2, yo, k, yo, ssk × 2, sl1, k2tog, psso, yo, k2tog, yo, k5. (22 sts)

Row 12: Bind off × 2, k3, p3tog, p2tog, p9, k2. (17 sts)

Row 13: Sl, k, (yo, k2tog) × 2, k2, yo, k3, yo, sl1, k2tog, psso, yo, k, yo × 2, k2. (20 sts)

Row 14: Repeat row 6.

Row 15: Sl, k, yo, k2tog, (yo, k2tog, k2) × 2, yo, k, yo, k2tog, yo, k5. (22 sts)

Row 16: Repeat row 8. (20 sts)

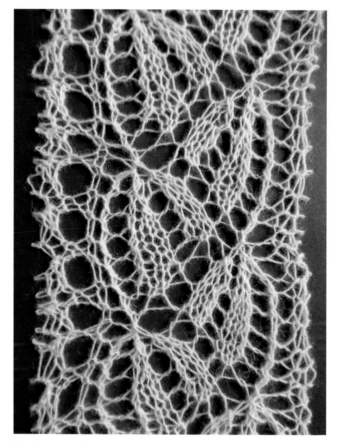

Day Flower border.

Day Flower border chart.

Edgings

Edgings are used to finish a knitted shawl or wrap. As with insertions and panels, however, they can equally be applied to knitted garments or accessories to very good effect.

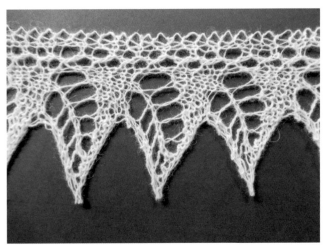

Fern Leaf edging.

Fern Leaf Edging

Fern Leaf edging also appears as Oak Leaf edging in places and is a very simple, easy to knit but effective edging. You can vary the size of the edging by adjusting the amount of increase rows knitted before the mass decrease. Just make sure that you cast off the same amount of stitches that you have added.

Fern Leaf Edging Instructions
Cast on 10 stitches.

Row 1 (RS): K2, yo, ssk, k, (yo × 2, k2tog) × 2, k. (12 sts)
Row 2 (WS): K3, p, k2, p, k, yo, p2tog, k2.
Row 3: K2, yo, ssk, k3, (yo × 2, k2tog) × 2, k. (14 sts)
Row 4: K3, p, k2, p, k3, yo, p2tog, k2.
Row 5: K2, yo, ssk, k5, (yo × 2, k2tog) × 2, k. (16 sts)
Row 6: K3, p, k2, p, k5, yo, p2tog, k2.
Row 7: K2, yo, ssk, k7, (yo × 2, k2tog) × 2, k. (18 sts)
Row 8: K3, p, k2, p, k7, yo, p2tog, k2.
Row 9: K2, yo, ssk, k9, (yo × 2, k2tog) × 2, k. (20 sts)
Row 10: K3, p, k2, p, k9, yo, p2tog, k2.
Row 11: K2, yo, ssk, k16.
Row 12: Bind off × 10, k6, yo, p2tog, k2. (10 sts)

Repeat these rows until the edging is to your desired length.

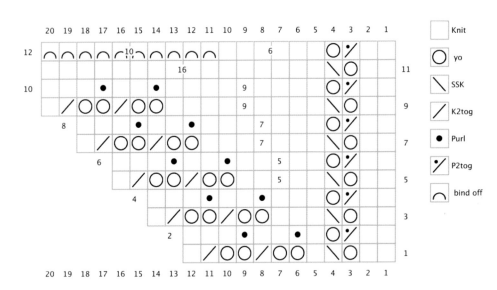

Fern Leaf edging chart.

Plain Vandyke

A pretty edging, and straightforward to knit. It looks good in thicker yarns as well as in finer yarn as here and would make a good edging for a blanket, for example.

Plain Vandyke Edging Instructions
Cast on 11 stitches.

Row 1 (RS): Sl, k2, (yo, k2tog) × 3, yo, k2. (12 sts)
Row 2 and all WS rows Sl, K
Row 3: Sl, k3, (yo, k2tog) × 3, yo, k2. (13 sts)
Row 5: Sl, k4, (yo, k2tog) × 3, yo, k2. (14 sts)
Row 7: Sl, k5, (yo, k2tog) × 3, yo, k2. (15 sts)
Row 9: Sl, k6, (yo, k2tog) × 3, yo, k2. (16 sts)
Row 11: Sl, k7, (yo, k2tog) × 3, yo, k2. (17 sts)
Row 13: Sl, k8, (yo, k2tog) × 3, yo, k2. (18 sts)
Row 15: Sl, k6, (ssk, yo) × 4, ssk, k. (17 sts)
Row 17: Sl, k5, (ssk, yo) × 4, ssk, k. (16 sts)
Row 19: Sl, k4, (ssk, yo) × 4, ssk, k. (15 sts)
Row 21: Sl, k3, (ssk, yo) × 4, ssk, k. (14 sts)
Row 23: Sl, k2, (ssk, yo) × 4, ssk, k. (13 sts)
Row 24: Repeat row 4.
Row 25: Sl, k, (ssk, yo) × 4, ssk, k. (12 sts)
Row 26: Repeat row 2.
Row 27: Sl, (ssk, yo) × 4, ssk, k. (11 sts)
Row 28: Sl, k10.

Repeat these rows until the edging is to your desired length.

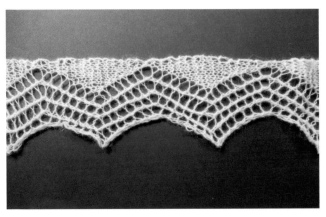

Plain Vandyke edging.

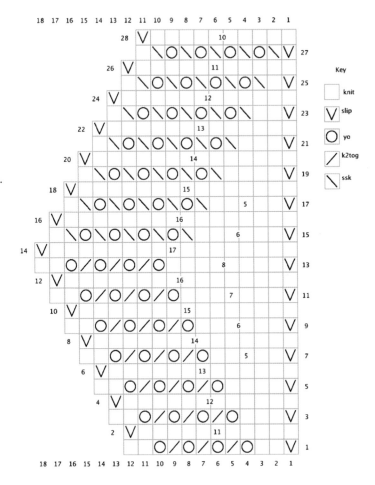

Plain Vandyke edging chart.

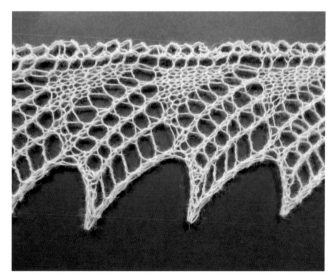
Coburg Lace edging.

Coburg Lace

This is another old lace edging, both attractive and versatile.

Coburg Lace Edging Instructions
Cast on 13 stitches.

Row 1 (RS): K, k2tog, yo, k, (yo, k2tog) × 3, yo × 2, k2tog, k. (14 sts)
Row 2 (WS): P3, k, p10.
Row 3: K, k2tog, yo, k2, (yo, k2tog) × 3, yo × 2, k2tog, k. (15 sts)
Row 4: P3, k, p11.
Row 5: K, k2tog, yo, k3, (yo, k2tog) × 3, yo × 2, k2tog, k. (16 sts)
Row 6: P3, k, p12.
Row 7: K, k2tog, yo, k4, (yo, k2tog) × 3, yo × 2, k2tog, k. (17 sts)
Row 8: Purl.
Row 9: K, k2tog, yo, k5, (yo, k2tog) × 3, yo × 2, k2tog, k. (18 sts)
Row 10: P3, k, p14.
Row 11: K, k2tog, yo, k6, (yo, k2tog) × 3, yo × 2, k2tog, k. (19 sts)
Row 12: P3, k, p15.
Row 13: K, k2tog, yo, k16.
Row 14: Bind off × 6, p13. (13 sts)

Repeat these rows until the edging is to your desired length.

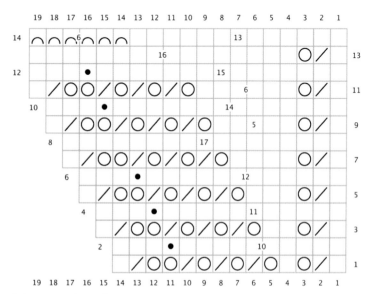

	knit
/	k2tog
○	yo
●	purl
⌒	bind off

Coburg Lace edging chart.

Traditional Peaked Lace

This pattern dates back to at least the mid 1880s. It is very pretty, straightforward to knit and was widely used in Victorian times to edge shawls.

Traditional Peaked Edging Instructions
Cast on 17 stitches.

Row 1 (RS): Sl, k, yo, ssk, k3, k2tog, yo, (k, yo, ssk) × 2, yo, k2. (18 sts)
Row 2 (WS): K15, yo, k2tog, k.
Row 3: Sl, k, yo, ssk, k2, k2tog, yo, k3, yo, ssk, k, yo, ssk, yo, k2. (19 sts)
Row 4: K16, yo, k2tog, k.
Row 5: Sl, k, yo, ssk, k, k2tog, yo, k5, yo, ssk, k, yo, ssk, yo, k2. (20 sts)
Row 6: K17, yo, k2tog, k.
Row 7: Sl, k, yo, ssk, k3, yo, ssk, k, k2tog, yo, k4, yo, ssk, yo, k2. (21 sts)
Row 8: K18, yo, k2tog, k.
Row 9: Sl, k, yo, ssk, k4, yo, sl1, k2tog, psso, yo, k6, yo, ssk, yo, k2. (22 sts)
Row 10: Bind off × 5, k14, yo, k2tog, k. (17 sts)

Repeat these rows until the edging is to your desired length.

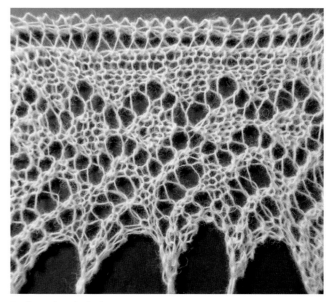

Traditional peaked edging.

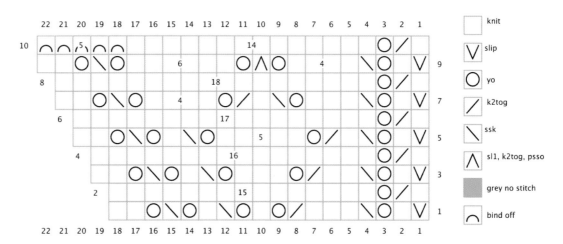

Traditional peaked edging chart.

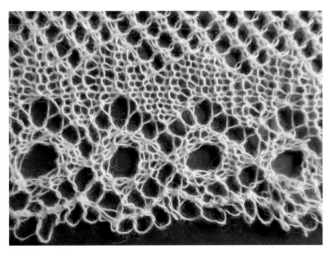

Irish Lace edging.

Irish, or Elaine Lace Edging

This is an old lace, which may or may not have originated in Ireland.

Irish Lace Edging Instructions

Cast on 20 stitches.

Row 1 (RS): Sl, k2, (ssk, yo) × 3, ssk, k3, k2tog, yo, k3, yo, k2. (21 sts)

Row 2 (WS): Yo, k2tog, k19.

Row 3: Sl, k3, (ssk, yo) × 2, ssk, k3, k2tog, yo, k5, yo, k2. (22 sts)

Row 4: Yo, k2tog, k20.

Row 5: Sl, k2, (ssk, yo) × 2, ssk, k3, k2tog, yo, ssk, k2tog, yo × 3, ssk, k, yo, k2. (23 sts)

Row 6: Yo, k2tog, k4, p, k16.

Row 7: Sl, k3, (ssk, yo) × 2, ssk, k4, yo, ssk, k3, k2tog, yo, k2tog, k2.

Row 8: Repeat row 4. (22 sts)

Row 9: Sl, k2, (ssk, yo) × 3, ssk, k4, yo, ssk, k, k2tog, yo, k2tog, k. (21 sts)

Row 10: Repeat row 2.

Row 11: Sl, k3, (ssk, yo) × 3, ssk, k4, yo, sl1, k2tog, psso, yo, k2tog, k. (20 sts)

Row 12: Yo, k2tog, k18.

Repeat these rows until the edging is to your desired length.

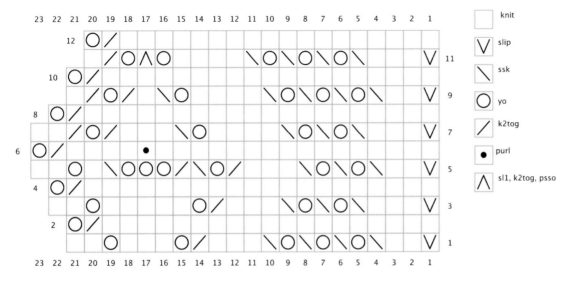

Irish Lace edging chart.

Cockleshell Lace

Another old lace. Don't be put off by the chart; it is very simple to knit and results in a softly pointed edging that bears a resemblance to cockleshells or scallop shells.

Cockleshell Lace Edging Instructions
Cast on 16 stitches plus 4 for garter band, 20 stitches.

Row 1 (RS): Sl, k3, yo, k2tog, k, yo, k10, yo, k2tog, k. (21 sts)
Row 2 (WS): k2, yo, k2tog, k17.
Row 3: Sl, k3, yo, k2tog, k, yo, k2tog, yo, k9, yo, k2tog, k. (22 sts)
Row 4: P2, yo, p2tog, p18.
Row 5: Sl, k3, yo, k2tog, k, (yo, k2tog) × 2, yo, k8, yo, k2tog, k. (23 sts)
Row 6: K2, yo, k2tog, k19.
Row 7: Sl, k3, yo, k2tog, k, (yo, k2tog) × 3, yo, k7, yo, k2tog, k. (24 sts)
Row 8: K2, yo, k2tog, k20.
Row 9: Sl, k3, yo, k2tog, k, (yo, k2tog) × 4, yo, k6, yo, k2tog, k. (25 sts)
Row 10: K2, yo, k2tog, k21.
Row 11: Sl, k3, yo, k2tog, k, (yo, k2tog) × 5, yo, k5, yo, k2tog, k. (26 sts)
Row 12: K2, yo, k2tog, k22.
Row 13: Sl, k3, yo, k2tog, k, (yo, k2tog) × 6, yo, k4, yo, k2tog, k. (27 sts)
Row 14: K2, yo, k2tog, k23.
Row 15: Sl, k3, yo, k2tog, k, (yo, k2tog) × 7, yo, k3, yo, k2tog, k. (28 sts)
Row 16: K2, yo, k2tog, k24.
Row 17: Sl, k3, yo, k2tog, (ssk, yo) × 7, ssk, k3, yo, k2tog, k. (27 sts)
Row 18: Repeat row 14.
Row 19: Sl, k3, yo, k2tog, (ssk, yo) × 6, ssk, k4, yo, k2tog, k. (26 sts)
Row 20: Repeat row 12.
Row 21: Sl, k3, yo, k2tog, (ssk, yo) × 5, ssk, k5, yo, k2tog, k. (25 sts)
Row 22: Repeat row 10.
Row 23: Sl, k3, yo, k2tog, (ssk, yo) × 4, ssk, k6, yo, k2tog, k. (24 sts)
Row 24: Repeat row 8.
Row 25: Sl, k3, yo, k2tog, (ssk, yo) × 3, ssk, k7, yo, k2tog, k. (23 sts)

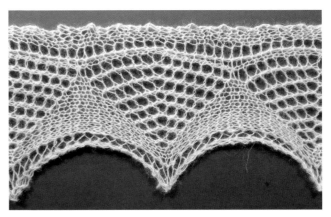

Cockleshell Lace edging.

Row 26: Repeat row 6.
Row 27: Sl, k3, yo, k2tog, (ssk, yo) × 2, ssk, k8, yo, k2tog, k. (22 sts)
Row 28: Repeat row 4.
Row 29: Sl, k3, yo, k2tog, ssk, yo, ssk, k9, yo, k2tog, k. (21 sts)
Row 30: Repeat row 2.
Row 31: Sl, k3, yo, k2tog, ssk, k10, yo, k2tog, k. (20 sts)
Row 32: K2, yo, k2tog, k16.

Repeat these rows until the edging is to your desired length.

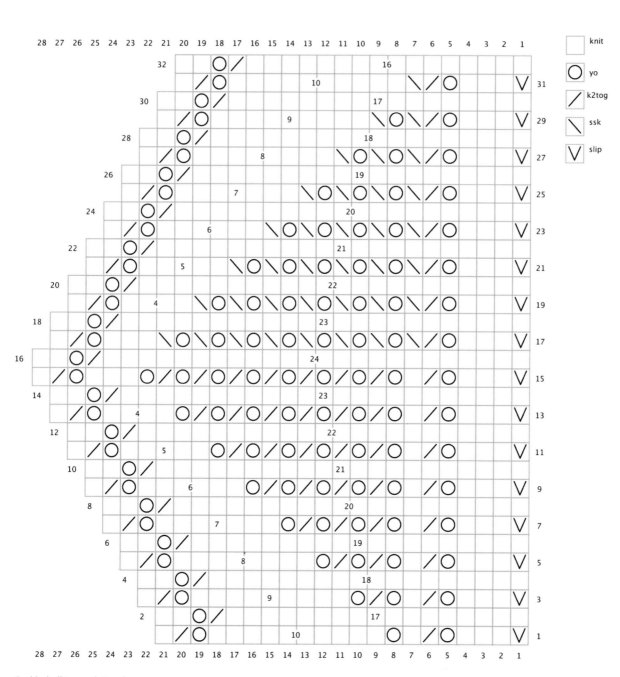

Cockleshell Lace edging chart.

Dainty Scalloped Lace Edging

This is a particularly dainty version of Scalloped Lace edging.

Dainty Scalloped Lace edging Instructions
Cast on 7 stitches.

Row 1: Set up row, do not repeat. (RS): Sl, k2, yo, k5, yo, ssk. (11 sts)
Row 2 (WS): Yo, k2tog, k9.
Row 3: Sl, k2, yo, k2tog, k, yo, k3, yo, ssk. (12 sts)
Row 4: Yo, k2tog, k10.
Row 5: Sl, k2, yo, k2tog, k, yo, k4, yo, ssk. (13 sts)
Row 6: Yo, k2tog, k11.
Row 7: Sl, k2, yo, k2tog, k, yo, k2tog, yo, k3, yo, ssk. (14 sts)
Row 8: Yo, k2tog, k12.
Row 9: Sl, k2, yo, k2tog, k, yo, k2tog, yo, k4, yo, ssk. (15 sts)
Row 10: Yo, k2tog, k13.
Row 11: Sl, k2, yo, k2tog, k, (yo, ssk) × 2, k3, yo, ssk.
Row 12: Yo, k2tog, k7, k2tog, k4. (14 sts)
Row 13: Sl, k2, yo, k2tog, k, (yo, ssk) × 2, k2, yo, ssk.
Row 14: Yo, k2tog, k6, k2tog, k4. (13 sts)
Row 15: Sl, k2, yo, k2tog, k, yo, ssk, k3, yo, ssk.
Row 16: Yo, k2tog, k5, k2tog, k4. (12 sts)
Row 17: Sl, k2, yo, k2tog, k, yo, ssk, k2, yo, ssk.
Row 18: Yo, (k2tog, k4) × 2. (11 sts)
Row 19: Sl, k2, yo, k2tog, k4, yo, ssk.
Row 20: Repeat row 2.
Row 21: Repeat row 19.

Repeat rows 2–21 until the edging is to desired length.

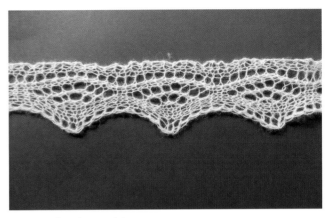

Dainty Scalloped Lace edging.

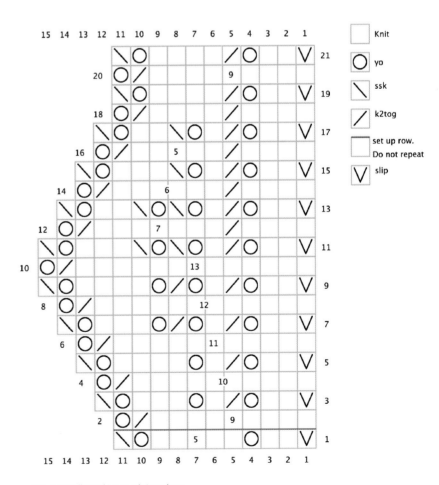

	Knit
O	yo
\	ssk
/	k2tog
	set up row. Do not repeat
V	slip

Dainty Scalloped Lace edging chart.

Wave edging.

Wave Edging

A lovely undulating edging that is easy to knit, and in this sample, by starting each row at the lace edge with a yarn over and knit 2 together, you get this an open edging which sets the pattern off beautifully.

Wave Lace Edging Instructions
Cast on 11 stitches.

Row 1 (RS): K3, yo, ssk, k2, yo, ssk, yo, k2. (12 sts)
Row 2 (WS): Yo, k2tog, k10.
Row 3: K2, (yo, ssk) × 2, k2, yo, ssk, yo, k2. (13 sts)
Row 4: Yo, k2tog, k11.
Row 5: K3, (yo, ssk) × 2, k2, yo, ssk, yo, k2. (14 sts)
Row 6: Yo, k2tog, k12.
Row 7: K2, (yo, ssk) × 3, k2, yo, ssk, yo, k2. (15 sts)
Row 8: Yo, k2tog, k13.
Row 9: (K2, (k2tog, yo) × 2) × 2, k2tog, k. (14 sts)
Row 10: Repeat row 6.
Row 11: K, (k2tog, yo) × 2, k2, (k2tog, yo) × 2, k2tog, k. (13 sts)
Row 12: Repeat row 4.
Row 13: (K2, k2tog, yo) × 2, k2tog, yo, k2tog, k. (12 sts)
Row 14: Repeat row 2.
Row 15: K, k2tog, yo, k2, (k2tog, yo) × 2, k2tog, k. (11 sts)
Row 16: Yo, k2tog, k9.

Repeat these rows until the edging is to desired length.

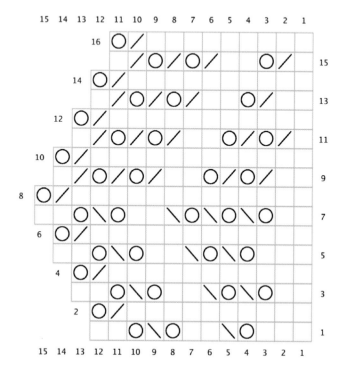

Wave edging chart.

	knit
O	yo
\	ssk
/	k2tog

Cyprus Edging

This is a very pretty lace edging, which requires some concentration but knit the chart as it is written, particularly row 6. There are six stitches before the yarn over, and you will need to knit and then purl into the double yarn over from the row before.

Cyprus Lace Edging Instructions
Cast on 12 stitches.

Row 1 (RS): Sl, k5, k2tog, yo, k, ssk, k. (11 sts)
Row 2 (WS): K4, yo, k2tog, k2, yo, k2tog, k.
Row 3: Sl, k3, k2tog, yo, k, ssk, k2. (10 sts)
Row 4: K7, yo, k2tog, k.
Row 5: Sl, k4, yo, ssk, k, yo × 2, k2. (12 sts)
Row 6: K3, p, k2, yo, k3, yo, k2tog, k. (13 sts)
Row 7: Sl, k6, yo, ssk, k4.
Row 8: Bind off × 2, k2, yo, k5, yo, k2tog, k. (11 sts)

Repeat these rows until the edging is to your desired length.

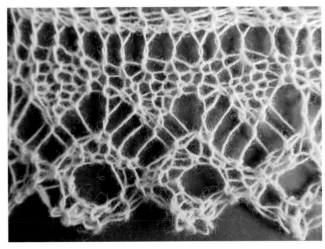

Cyprus edging.

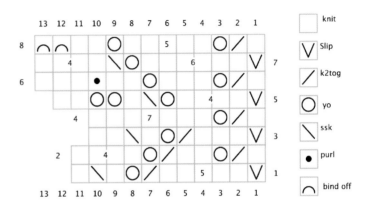

Cyprus edging chart.

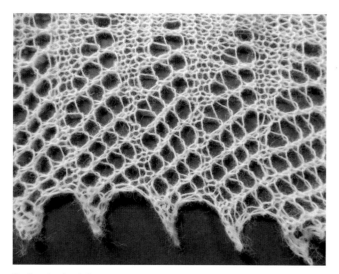

Godmother's edging.

Godmother's Edging, or Margaret's Edging

This is an old Victorian pattern of which there appears to be various versions. It is very straightforward to knit and gives a surprisingly attractive edging.

Godmother's Edging Instructions
Cast on 20 stitches.

Row 1 (RS): Sl, k3, (yo, k2tog) × 7, yo, k2. (21 sts)
Row 2 (WS): Knit.
Row 3: Sl, k6, (yo, k2tog) × 6, yo, k2. (22 sts)
Row 4: Knit.
Row 5: Sl, k9, (yo, k2tog) × 5, yo, k2. (23 sts)
Row 6: Knit.
Row 7: Sl, k12, (yo, k2tog) × 4, yo, k2. (24 sts)
Row 8: Knit.
Row 9: Sl, k23.
Row 10: Bind off × 4, k20. (20 sts)

Repeat these rows until the edging is to your desired length.

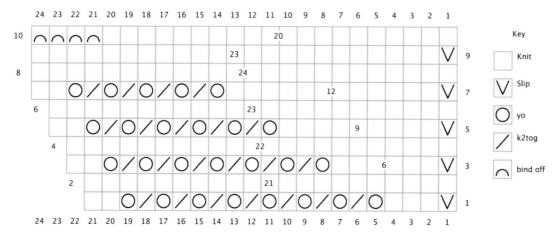

Godmother's edging chart.

Estonian stitch patterns

Included here are a couple of the better known Estonian Lace stitches, in order to provide a little insight into some of the differences in technique used by knitters in this tradition. There are many more motifs and patterns than shown here and if you are interested in Estonian Lace, then I have included some sources of further information in the bibliography at the end of the book.

Estonian Star Stitch

This very attractive all over motif is frequently used as a filler in Estonian patterns. It is so pretty that it is more than capable of standing on its own as an all over pattern. This version is a make two stitches from two, however, make three stitches from three is also widely used. This version is particularly dainty and works very well in a fine yarn.

Star Stitch written instructions
Row 1 (RS): K1, 2-2 tbl x 9, k1. (20 sts)
Row 2 and all WS rows: Purl.
Row 3: K2, 2-2 tbl x 9.
Row 5: Repeat row 1.

Special Instructions
2–2 makes 2 stitches from 2 stitches.
Knit 2 together front and back. Two stitches from 2.

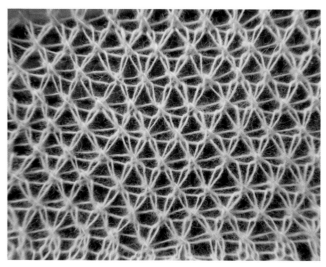

Estonian Star stitch.

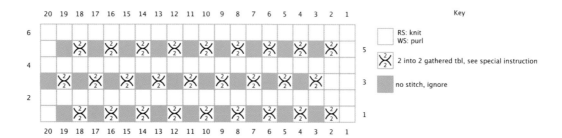

Estonian Star stitch chart.

Key

RS: knit
WS: purl

2 into 2 gathered tbl, see special instruction

no stitch, ignore

Estonian Flower Stitch

This is an especially attractive stitch in Estonian knitting, although any search of the internet will soon have you wondering what this pattern actually is as it is variously described as Star stitch, Flower stitch and Waterlily. It is included here because it is so pretty, although the make nine stitches from three increase may require a little practice. Study the chart carefully before starting the knit.

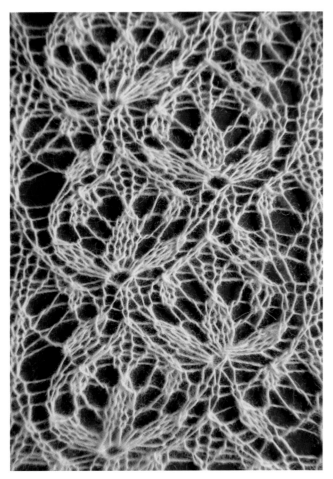
Estonian Flower stitch.

Estonian Flower Stitch Instructions

Row 1 (RS): Sl, k6, yo, sl1, k2tog, psso, yo, k9, yo, ssk, k2. (23 sts)

Row 2 (WS): Sl wyif, p25. (26 sts)

Row 3: Sl, k2, yo, incto3 tbl, sl1, k2tog, psso, k3, sl1, k2tog, psso, k, incto9 tbl, k, sl1, k2tog, psso, k4. (28 sts)

Row 4: Repeat row 2. (26 sts)

Row 5: Sl, k3, yo, k3, ssk, k, k2tog, (k3, yo) × 2, k3, ssk, k3.

Row 6: Repeat row 2.

Row 7: Sl, k3, yo, k, yo, sl1, k2tog, psso × 3, yo, k, yo, k3, yo, k, yo, sl1, k2tog, psso, ssk, k2. (23 sts)

Row 8: Sl wyif, p27. (28 sts)

Row 9: Sl, k, k2tog, yo, k9, yo, sl1, k2tog, psso, yo, k7. (23 sts)

Row 10: Repeat row 2. (26 sts)

Row 11: Sl, k3, sl1, k2tog, psso, k, incto9 tbl, k, sl1, k2tog, psso, k3, sl1, k2tog, psso, incto3 tbl, yo, k3. (28 sts)

Row 12: Sl wyif, p26. (27 sts)

Row 13: Sl, k2, k2tog, (k3, yo) × 2, k3, ssk, k, k2tog, k3, yo, k4. (26 sts)

Row 14: Repeat row 2.

Row 15: Sl, k, k2tog, sl1, k2tog, psso, yo, k, yo, k3, yo, k, yo, sl1, k2tog, psso × 3, yo, k, yo, k4. (23 sts)

Special Instructions
incto3 tbl

This is an increase of one stitch to three.

To do this, knit front and back then front again, then slip the left-hand stitch off the needle. Three stitches created.

incto9 tbl

This is an increase from three stitches to nine.

Insert the right-hand needle into three stitches on the left-hand needle as if to knit 3 together. Wrap the yarn around and pull the loop through as if knitting, but do not slip off the needle. Next do a yarn over and then knit into the stitches again without slipping the three stitches off the needle. Repeat the yarn over and knit until you have nine stitches on the right-hand needle. Now slip the three stitches from the left-hand needle off.

When purling back on the next wrong side row, take care to ensure that you work the increased stitches in the right order.

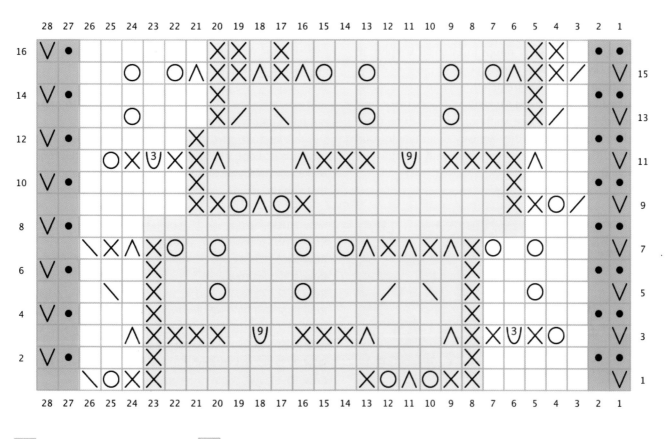

RS: knit
WS: purl

RS: k2tog
WS: p2tog

no stitch, ignore these

edge stitches

yo

RS: slip
WS: slip purlwise with yarn in front

RS: sl1, k2tog, psso
WS: sl1 wyif, p2tog tbl, psso

12 st 16 row repeat

RS: ssk
WS: p2tog tbl

side sts

inc 3 to 9, see note

RS: purl
WS: knit

inc 1 to 3 tbl

Estonian Flower stitch chart.

Lily of the Valley

This motif typifies the use of nupps in Estonian knitting. It emulates the Lily of the Valley pattern of which there are many versions. These bobbles are frequently seen in lace but are also used to add texture to regular knitting. Nupps make very attractive bobbles in fine lace knitting, and once you have mastered their construction, they are easy to include in your own designs. Think about combining them with Star stitch as a background.

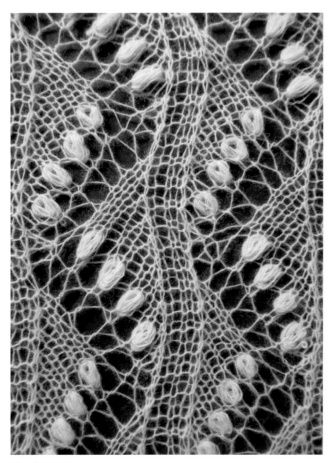

Lily of the Valley.

Lily of the Valley Instructions

This pattern is worked over multiples of twenty-two stitches, plus six edge stitches. It is a twenty-four row pattern repeat.

The nupps are a nine stitch nupp. This means that you will be increasing one stitch to nine where the nupp is indicated. Please refer to the detailed instructions on how to make this nupp in Chapter 3 – Techniques.

On the return row, you will be decreasing the nine stitch nupp back to one stitch by purling the nine stitches together. Make sure that you capture all of the stitches, and similarly that you do not inadvertently knit extra stitches by mistake.

Row 1 (RS): Sl, (k2, ssk, k5, yo, k, yo, k2tog) × 2, k3. (28 sts)
Row 2 (WS): Sl wyif, (k2, p10) × 2, k3.
Row 3: Sl, (k2, ssk, k4, (yo, k) × 2, k2tog) × 2, k3.
Row 4: Repeat row 2.
Row 5: Sl, (k2, ssk, k3, yo, k, yo, nupp, k, k2tog) × 2, k3.
Row 6: Sl wyif, (k2, p2, dec9to1, p7) × 2, k3.
Row 7: Sl, (k2, ssk, k2, yo, k, yo, nupp, k2, k2tog) × 2, k3.
Row 8: Sl wyif, (k2, p3, dec9to1, p6) × 2, k3.
Row 9: Sl, (k2, ssk, (k, yo) × 2, nupp, k3, k2tog) × 2, k3.
Row 10: Sl wyif, (k2, p4, dec9to1, p5) × 2, k3.
Row 11: Sl, (k2, ssk, yo, k, yo, nupp, k4, k2tog) × 2, k3.
Row 12: Sl wyif, (k2, p5, dec9to1, p4) × 2, k3.
Row 13: Sl, k3, yo, k, yo, k5, k2tog, k2, ssk, yo, k, yo, k5, k2tog, k3.
Row 14: Repeat row 2.
Row 15: Sl, k4, yo, k, yo, k4, k2tog, k2, ssk, (k, yo) × 2, k4, k2tog, k3.
Row 16: Repeat row 2.
Row 17: Sl, k4, nupp, yo, k, yo, k3, k2tog, k2, ssk, k, nupp, yo, k, yo, k3, k2tog, k3.
Row 18: Sl wyif, (k2, p7, dec9to1, p2) × 2, k3.
Row 19: Sl, k5, nupp, yo, k, yo, k2, k2tog, k2, ssk, k2, nupp, yo, k, yo, k2, k2tog, k3.
Row 20: Sl wyif, (k2, p6, dec9to1, p3) × 2, k3.
Row 21: Sl, k6, nupp, (yo, k) × 2, k2tog, k2, ssk, k3, nupp, (yo, k) × 2, k2tog, k3.
Row 22: Repeat row 12.
Row 23: Sl, k7, nupp, yo, k, yo, k2tog, k2, ssk, k4, nupp, yo, k, yo, k2tog, k3.
Row 24: Repeat row 10.

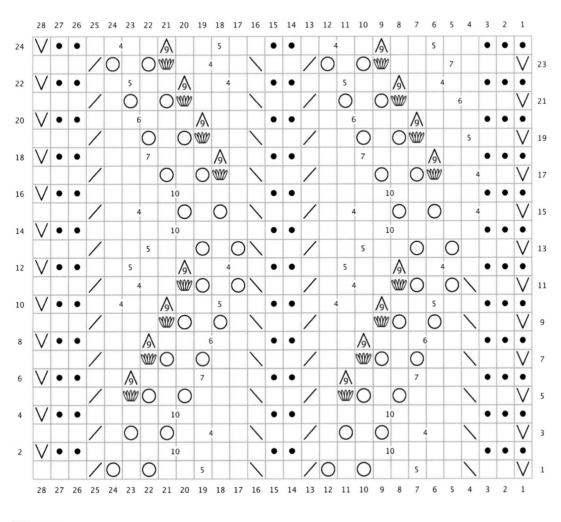

☐	RS: knit WS: purl	

RS: knit
WS: purl

RS: ssk
WS: p2tog tbl

yo

RS: k2tog
WS: p2tog

9 st nupp

decrease 9 to 1

RS: purl
WS: knit

RS: slip
WS: slip purlwise with yarn in front

Lily of the Valley chart.

Orenburg lace

Knitted samples of each of the basic patterns for this lace tradition are not included, because taken on their own they are not necessarily very inspiring, with the magic of Orenburg Lace being the intricate and highly complex way in which these comparatively simple motifs are put together to create truly beautiful lace. It falls outside the remit of this book to provide detailed instruction as to how to create this lace, however, I have included the charts for each of the basic stitches used so that an understanding of the basic motifs can be gained. There are pointers for finding additional information about this lace tradition at the end of the book.

A modern day example of Orenburg lace.

Diagonals

Diagonals Instructions
Row 1 (RS): K2, (yo, k2tog) × 3, k2. (10 sts)
Row 2 and all WS rows: Knit.
Row 3: K3, (yo, k2tog) × 2, k3.
Row 5: K4, yo, k2tog, k4.

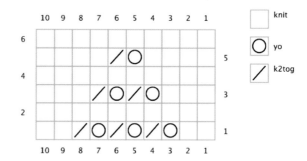

Diagonals chart.

Fish Eyes

Fish Eyes Instructions
Row 1 (RS): K3, (yo, k2tog, k5) × 2, yo, k2tog, k3. (22 sts)
Row 2 (WS): (P, yo, p2tog, p2, yo, p2tog) × 3, p.
Row 3: Repeat row 1.

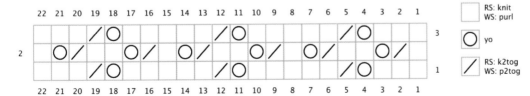

Fish Eyes chart.

Honeycomb

Honeycomb Instructions
Row 1 (RS): Knit. (10 sts)
Row 2 (WS): Knit.
Row 3: K4, yo, k2tog, k4.
Row 4: K4, yo, k2tog, k4.
Row 5: (K2, yo, k2tog) × 2, k2.
Row 6: (K2, yo, k2tog) × 2, k2.
Row 7: Repeat row 3.
Row 8: Repeat row 4.
Row 9: Knit.
Row 10: Knit.

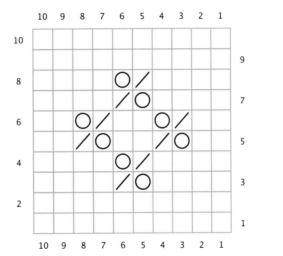

Honeycomb chart.

Mouse Prints

Mouse Prints Instructions
Row 1 (RS): K3, yo, k2tog, k7, yo, k2tog, k3. (17 sts)
Row 2 and all WS rows: Knit.
Row 3: K2, (yo, k2tog) × 2, k5, (yo, k2tog) × 2, k2.
Row 5: Repeat row 1.

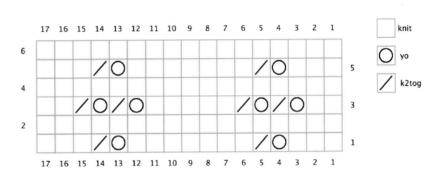

Mouse Prints chart.

Orenburg Cat's Paw

Orenburg Cat's Paw Instructions
Row 1 (RS): K4, (yo, k2tog) × 2, k9, (yo, k2tog) × 2, k4.
  (25 sts)
Row 2 and all WS rows: Knit.
Row 3: K3, (yo, k2tog) × 3, k7, (yo, k2tog) × 3, k3.
Row 5: Repeat row 1.

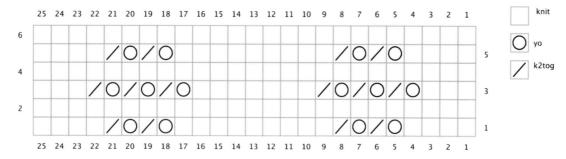

Orenburg Cat's Paw chart.

Peas

Peas Instructions
Row 1 (RS): Knit. (24 sts)
Row 2 (WS): Knit.
Row 3: K4, (yo, k2tog, k2) × 5.
Row 4: K4, (yo, k2tog, k2) × 5.
Row 5: Knit.
Row 6: Knit,
Row 7: (K2, yo, k2tog) × 5, k4.
Row 8: (K2, yo, k2tog) × 5, k4.

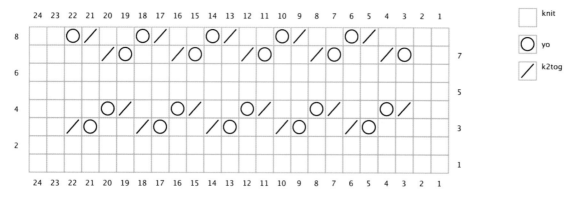

Peas chart.

Strawberry

Strawberry Instructions
Row 1 (RS): K4, (yo, k2tog) × 2, k9, (yo, k2tog) × 2, k4. (25 sts)
Row 2 and all WS rows: Knit.
Row 3: K2, yo, k2tog, k4, yo, k2tog, k5, yo, k2tog, k4, yo, k2tog, k2.
Row 5: K4, yo, k3tog, yo, k10, yo, k3tog, yo, k5.

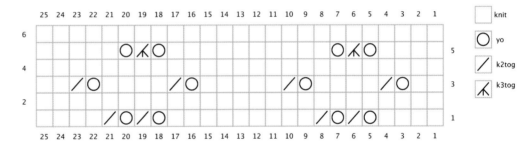

Strawberry chart.

The Accordion

The Accordion Instructions
Row 1 and all RS rows: K3, (k2tog, yo) × 3, k3.
Row 2 (WS): K3, (k2tog, yo) × 3, k3. (12 sts)
Row 4: Repeat row 2.
Row 6: Repeat row 2.
Row 8: Knit.

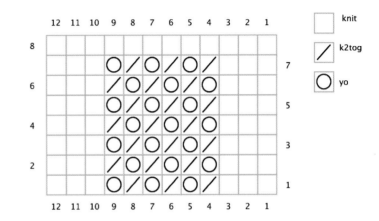

The Accordion chart.

Chain Hearts

Chain Hearts Instructions
Row 1 (RS): K7, yo, k2tog, k6. (15 sts)
Row 2 and all WS rows: Knit.
Row 3: K5, k2tog, yo, k, yo, k2tog, k5.
Row 5: K4, k2tog, yo, k3, yo, k2tog, k4.
Row 7: K3, k2tog, yo, k5, yo, k2tog, k3.
Row 9: K2, k2tog, yo, k3, (yo, k2tog, k2) × 2.
Row 11: K4, yo, k3tog, yo, k, yo, k3tog, yo, k4.

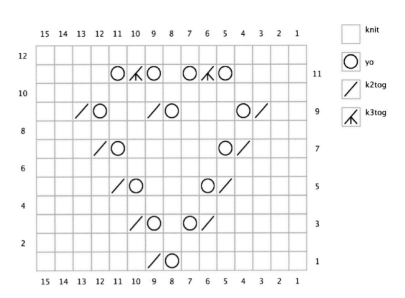

Chain Hearts chart.

CHAPTER 5

EDGINGS AND EMBELLISHMENTS

Although lace knitting can appear daunting and appears to have something of a mystique about it, it is not so difficult. Providing you are able to increase, decrease, knit and purl, you should have no problems completing the majority of the lace knitting patterns contained within this book and elsewhere. As with any knitting patterns, there are some special techniques that are generally explained by the writer of the pattern. Some patterns will require more concentration than others, and all will need you to keep check of the number of stitches to ensure that you have neither lost nor gained more than you should have.

With practice, it becomes easier to 'read' your stitches whilst knitting, and thus easier to check what has gone wrong if at the end of a row you have the wrong number of stitches, or the right number of stitches but the pattern not lining up as it should. It is important to keep checking as you go; using life lines is an invaluable aid in the event that it proves necessary to take work back to a point at which everything was right, or if a stitch has been lost and finding it has eluded you.

Lace is knitted on a background of either garter stitch or stocking stitch, effectively providing the canvas for the lace stitches.

Some lace has a right and wrong side, and some is the same on both sides. Shetland lace was traditionally knitted on a garter stitch ground as was Orenburg lace, thus making it easier and quicker to knit the patterns. The advantage of this approach is not only the fact of not being slowed by having to purl, but also lace that does not have an obvious wrong side.

Other lace traditions use predominantly stocking stitch grounds, thus requiring alternate rows of purl knitting and lace that has a much more obvious right and wrong side. It is interesting to observe that in the case of the Shetland pattern Old Shell, it was a garter stitch pattern. Any cursory search of the internet, however, will produce predominantly a pattern for this that includes a purl row as follows:

Row 1: knit.
Row 2: purl.
Row 3: (k2tog x3 (yo, k1) x 6, k2tog x 3) to end of row
Row 4: knit.

Old Shell incorporating a purl row.

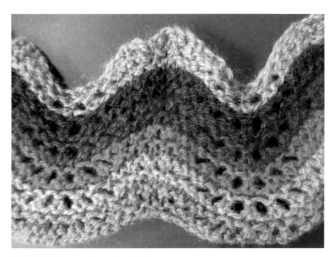

Old Shell using only garter stitch.

Thus, the pattern that includes a row of purl, and which does indeed produce an attractive version of this pattern, has a wrong side and a right side. The garter stitch version does not. This is not an uncommon observation with many of the stitch patterns attributed to the Shetland tradition.

Some patterns may work very well in garter stitch; however, others may lose some of their clarity, whilst others may only work in stocking stitch. Again, it is always worth experimenting to see whether changes in the stitch used as the background will work in a particular design.

Some lace has pattern stitches on only alternate rows, thus providing in effect a rest row in between, whilst others are patterned on both sides, and require full focus without the luxury of the occasional rest row!

Using Eyelets to Create Original Personal Patterns

Creating lace patterns with eyelets is the simple expedient of pairing a yarn over with a decrease. This creates an eyelet. It is easy to place eyelets anywhere you wish, and patterns, often complex ones, can be created using this approach.

Eyelets differ from knitted lace in that there is more fabric and fewer holes, and the holes are spaced out to create the pattern, whereas with knitted lace there is less fabric and more holes. Eyelets that are made too close together result in Faggot lace.

You will need to think about the direction of the decrease that you are pairing with your yarn over: should it be left or right leaning? Knit 2 together results in a lean to the right, whereas ssk, skp and knit 2 together tbl all result in a lean to the left.

If you study the chart of the Eyelet Diamond Pattern later in this chapter, you will observe that the direction of lean changes with the slant of the diamond, with the decreases mirroring each other to provide balance to the finished pattern. If you keep this in mind when designing eyelet patterns you should have no difficulty producing balanced motifs.

It is really easy to design eyelet patterns, and plotting the pattern on some squared paper or stitch related graph paper allows you to plan how the pattern will look when it is knitted.

Rows of eyelets can be used for edgings, for creating a focal point in an otherwise plain knit garment or as more elaborate all over patterns.

This is an attractive border pattern that would work well around cuffs, the bottom of a sweater, along the side of a band or repeated at intervals as a pattern in its own right.

On an odd number of stitches on a ground of stocking stitch, the order of knitting for this is:

Row 1: RS, knit
Row 2: WS, knit
Row 3: k2tog, yo, to end, k 1
Row 4: knit.

Eyelet Diamonds

Eyelet Diamond written instruction

Row 1 (RS): K3, k2tog, (yo, k5, yo, sl1, k2tog, psso) × 2, yo, k5, yo, ssk, k3. (31 sts)
Row 2 and all WS rows: Purl.
Row 3: K4, (yo, ssk, k3, k2tog, yo, k1) × 2, yo, ssk, k3, k2tog, yo, k4.
Row 5: K5, (yo, ssk, k1, k2tog, yo, k3) × 2, yo, ssk, k1, k2tog, yo, k5.
Row 7: K6, (yo, sl1, k2tog, psso, yo, k5) × 2, yo, sl1, k2tog, psso, yo, k6.
Row 9: K5, (k2tog, yo, k1, yo, ssk, k3) × 2, k2tog, yo, k1, yo, ssk, k5.
Row 11: K4, (k2tog, yo, k3, yo, ssk, k1) × 2, k2tog, yo, k3, yo, ssk, k4.
Row 13: Repeat row 1.
Row 15: Repeat row 3.
Row 17: Repeat row 5.
Row 19: Repeat row 7.
Row 21: Repeat row 9.
Row 23: Repeat row 11.

Eyelet Diamonds.

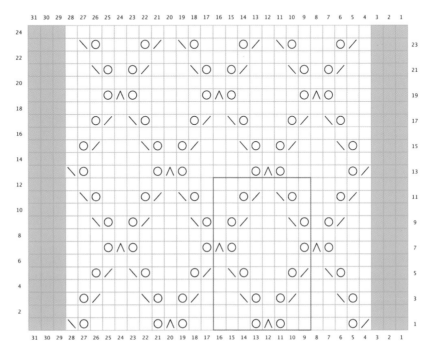

Eyelet Diamonds chart.

Zigzag Eyelets.

Zigzag Eyelets

Zigzag Eyelets Instructions
Row 1 (RS): K6, (k2tog, yo, k3) × 3, k2tog, yo, k5. (28 sts)
Row 2 and all WS rows: Purl.
Row 3: K5, (k2tog, yo, k3) × 3, k2tog, yo, k6.
Row 5: K4, (k2tog, yo, k3) × 3, k2tog, yo, k7.
Row 7: (K3, k2tog, yo) × 4, k8.
Row 9: K5, (yo, ssk, k3) × 3, yo, ssk, k6.
Row 11: K6, (yo, ssk, k3) × 3, yo, ssk, k5.
Row 13: K7, (yo, ssk, k3) × 3, yo, ssk, k4.
Row 15: K8, (yo, ssk, k3) × 4.
Row 17: Repeat row 1.
Row 19: Repeat row 3.
Row 21: Repeat row 5.
Row 23: Repeat row 7.

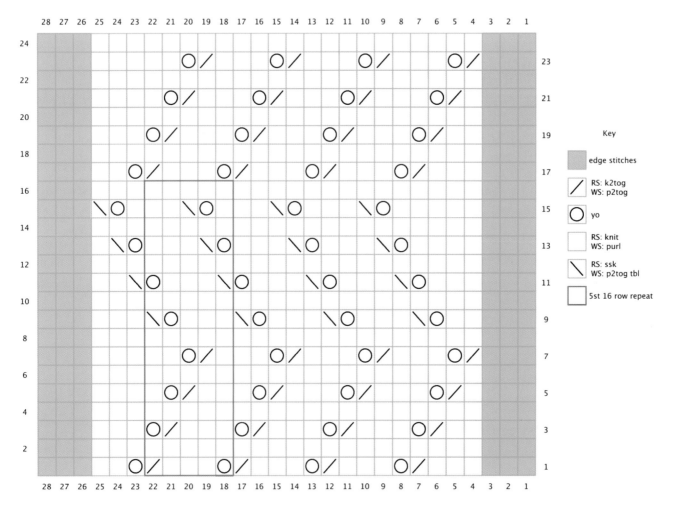

Key

▨	edge stitches
╱	RS: k2tog WS: p2tog
◯	yo
▢	RS: knit WS: purl
╲	RS: ssk WS: p2tog tbl
▭	5st 16 row repeat

Zigzag Eyelets chart.

Eyelet Twigs

Eyelet Twigs Instructions

Row 1 (RS): K3, (k2tog, yo, k, yo, ssk, k7) × 2, k2tog, yo, k, yo, ssk, k6. (38 sts)

Row 2 and all WS rows: Purl.

Row 3: K7, (yo, ssk, k10) × 2, yo, ssk, k5.

Row 5: K8, (yo, ssk, k10) × 2, yo, ssk, k4.

Row 7: K6, (k2tog, yo, k, yo, ssk, k7) × 2, k2tog, yo, k, yo, ssk, k3.

Row 9: (K5, k2tog, yo, k3, yo, ssk) × 3, k2.

Row 11: K4, (k2tog, yo, k10) × 2, k2tog, yo, k8.

Row 13: Repeat row 1.

Row 15: Repeat row 3.

Row 17: Repeat row 5.

Row 19: Repeat row 7.

Row 21: Repeat row 9.

Row 23: Repeat row 11.

Row 25: Repeat row 1.

Eyelet Twigs.

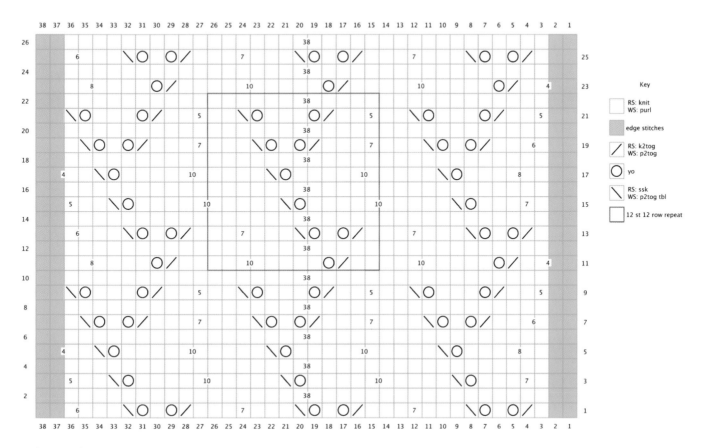

Eyelet Twigs chart.

Eyelet Chevrons with Bobbles

Eyelet Chevron with Bobbles Instructions

Row 1 (RS): (K3, yo, ssk) × 2, k5, k2tog, yo, k3, k2tog, yo, k, yo, ssk, k3, yo, ssk, k5, (k2tog, yo, k3) × 2. (45 sts)

Row 2 and all WS rows: Purl.

Row 3: K4, (yo, ssk, k3) × 2, (k2tog, yo, k3) × 2, (yo, ssk, k3) × 2, k2tog, yo, k3, k2tog, yo, k4.

Row 5: (K5, yo, ssk, k3, yo, ssk, mb, k2tog, yo, k3, k2tog, yo) × 2, k5.

Row 7: K6, yo, ssk, k9, k2tog, yo, k7, yo, ssk, k9, k2tog, yo, k6.

Row 9: K7, yo, ssk, k7, k2tog, yo, k9, yo, ssk, k7, k2tog, yo, k7.

Row 11: K8, yo, ssk, k5, k2tog, yo, k11, yo, ssk, k5, k2tog, yo, k8.

Row 13: K9, yo, ssk, k3, k2tog, yo, k13, yo, ssk, k3, k2tog, yo, k9.

Row 15: K10, yo, ssk, mb, k2tog, yo, k15, yo, ssk, mb, k2tog, yo, k10.

Row 17: Repeat row 1.

Row 19: Repeat row 3.

Row 21: Repeat row 5.

Row 23: Repeat row 7.

Row 25: Repeat row 9.

Row 27: Repeat row 11.

Row 29: Repeat row 13.

Row 31: Repeat row 15.

Eyelet Chevron with bobbles.

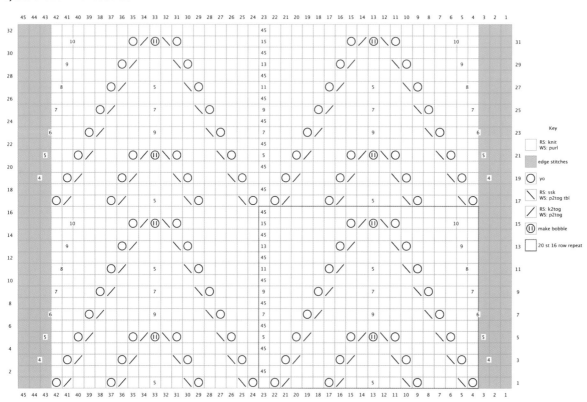

Eyelet Chevron with bobbles chart.

Pineapple Flower Eyelet Lace

Pineapple Flower Eyelet Lace Instructions

Row 1 (RS): K2, k2tog, yo, k5, yo, ssk, k2. (13 sts)

Row 2 and all WS rows: Purl.

Row 3: K3, yo, ssk, k3, k2tog, yo, k3.

Row 5: K5, yo, sl1, k2tog, psso, yo, k5.

Row 7: K3, k2tog, yo, k3, yo, ssk, k3.

Row 9: Repeat row 1.

Row 11: Repeat row 3.

Row 13: Repeat row 5.

Why not try putting together an eyelet motif of your own on some squared paper, and perhaps try combining eyelets with some bobbles?

If you are new to lace knitting, a good way to get started is to knit some swatches. Why not try some of the motifs from the Stitchionary? Try knitting them in thicker yarn and then use a crochet hook to join them together. You could make a lovely sampler which you could use as a throw and get some practice with the stitches at the same time. Choose an edging to attach at the end.

You can if you wish add texture and embellishment to lace with the addition of bobbles or beads or indeed cables, samples of which can be found in the Stitchionary. Estonian lace is particularly known for its 'bobble', and the nupp, which is used to create definition and outlines in many of the traditional patterns, is a particularly attractive manifestation of this.

Lace can be effectively combined with cables, not only the combinations that are included in the Stitchionary, but by including lace panels and inserts with a wide range of cable patterns to create interest and texture. This is fun to explore and experiment with.

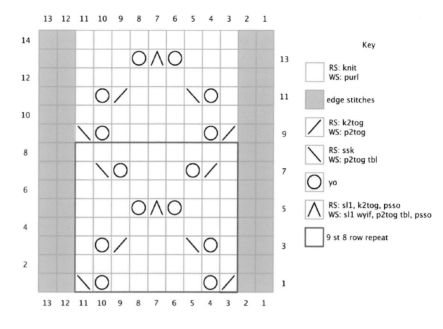

Key

☐	RS: knit / WS: purl
▩	edge stitches
╱	RS: k2tog / WS: p2tog
╲	RS: ssk / WS: p2tog tbl
◯	yo
⋀	RS: sl1, k2tog, psso / WS: sl1 wyif, p2tog tbl, psso
☐	9 st 8 row repeat

Pineapple Flower Eyelet Lace chart.

Pineapple Flower Eyelet Lace pattern.

Lace motifs knitted in DK Merino and then crocheted together to start a blanket.

Chart your ideas on some squared paper before starting the knit.

Bobbles

Bobbles are versatile and easy to insert into an existing pattern. They create interest and texture and can be used to provide outlines for patterns and motifs. If you want to insert bobbles into a design, try plotting their placement on squared paper before beginning the knitting so that you have a clear picture of how they will look and where they need to be placed.

Bobbles can be placed anywhere you want and often work well in conjunction with eyelet lace.

The term MB in knitting patterns indicates that you should make a bobble, and the number after it denotes how many times you should knit and purl into the stitch where the bobble is to be made.

Make a Bobble

MB1

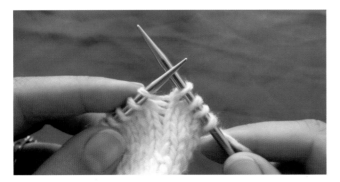

Knit to one stitch before the bobble.

Knit and purl into the next stitch twice.

Pass the second, third, and then fourth stitch over the first.

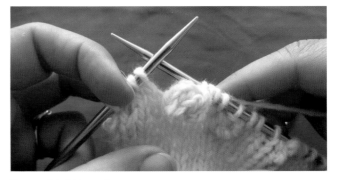

One small bobble made.

MB2

Repeat steps one and two as for MB1.

One slightly larger bobble made.

Knit and purl twice into the same stitch then turn the work and purl the stitches just increased.

Turn the work again and knit and then purl just those increased stitches for two rows. With the right side facing, decrease by slipping two stitches, knitting two stitches together and then passing the two slipped stitches over.

MB3

Knit to one stitch before the bobble. Knit and purl twice into the stitch, turn, and purl four, turn, knit four, turn, purl four, then with right side facing slip two stitches, knit 2 together and then pass the slipped stitches over. One large bobble made.

Big Bobble, MB3; Middle Bobble MB2; Small bobble, MB1.

This is not the only method of making bobbles and as previously mentioned, the Estonian tradition has its own very recognizable bobble known as the nupp. The use of the nupp in Estonian knitted lace creates a very lovely textured effect.

The nupp is created by knitting into one stitch, leaving it on the left-hand needle, then making a yarn over, knitting into same stitch again, several times, very loosely, and finishing by knitting the stitch.

Make a Nupp

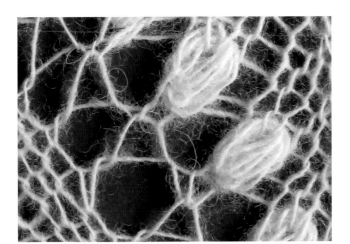

Example of the Estonian nupp.

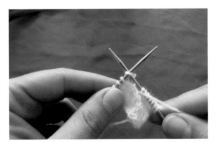

Knit to one stitch before the nupp. Knit into the next stitch but leave it on the left-hand needle. Now do a yarn over.

Now knit into the same stitch again and leave it on the left-hand needle and repeat the yarn over.

Repeat this process until you have the desired number of stitches, usually five, seven or nine on the right-hand needle. Now slip the stitch off. On the right-hand needle there is now a multiple increase of five, seven or nine stitches.

It is really important that the nupp yarn overs are loose, but also even, so try putting your needle into the completed nupp on the right side row and give it a good tug before moving on to the next stitch.

On the return wrong side row you will work as indicated by the pattern to the nupp.

People do sometimes find nupps a bit of a challenge, however, the art is in creating a nupp that is even, and loose enough to be able to get your needle into on the return row, and that is then correctly knitted back. With fine yarn, it may be difficult sometimes to see exactly where the nupp begins so count back the stitches to the nupp, and then count the nupp loops before you knit them to be sure you have not missed any, or included stitches that should not be in the nupp.

Making nupps needs a little practice, but is worth persevering with as the results are very attractive.

Purl the nupp stitch with the wraps together, reducing the stitch back to its original one.

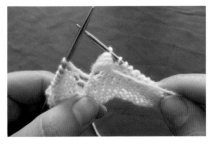

The nupp has now been taken back to the original stitch.

The completed nupp.

Beads

Adding beads to lace is not difficult to do, but does require a little planning. Where the beads are to be placed, how frequently this will occur and which method of placement you will use are all-important considerations. It may be helpful to plot the bead placements on a chart before beginning.

There are two main methods of placing beads, pre-stringing and placement with a crochet hook.

If you want to use a lot of beads then stringing them all onto the yarn before starting may not be the most practical approach, it is also quite time consuming. In addition the beads will eventually weaken the yarn as they are slid into position and can result in the yarn breaking. In this case, a decision will need to be made as to whether it is better to thread smaller quantities of the beads, and then break the yarn periodically but in a planned way to re-thread another batch, or whether using a crochet hook to place the beads is the more practical approach.

The two different approaches result in slightly different ways of securing the beads in place, and produce slightly different finished results. Depending upon the pattern, you will need to decide which method is likely to provide the best results as well as being the most practical.

Placing a Bead Using the Threaded Bead Method
Having once threaded the required number of beads onto your working yarn, knit across the right side row to the stitch where you wish to place a bead.

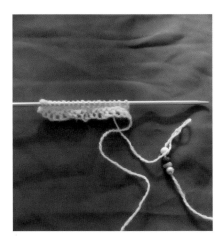

Thread the beads onto the yarn in the order in which they are to be used.

Bring the yarn round to the front of the work and then slip the next stitch knitwise.

Push the bead into position, and then bring the yarn round to the back of the work. It is advisable to check the bead at this point to make sure it is placed correctly.

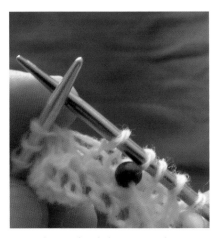

Knit to the next bead placement and repeat this process.

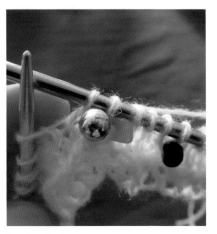

Two beads placed.

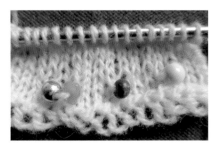

Two beads placed together. This picture also shows the little bars that are created by this method of bead placement.

This approach allows you to place more than one bead at a time if you wish, by slipping more than one stitch, for example, placing two or three beads over two slipped stitches. You can also place beads more loosely so that they hang down in little curves.

The stability of the bead placement largely depends on the tension of the bar where the bead is placed.

Whilst this approach allows for a degree of versatility, and works beautifully when beads are used to replace nupps in this Estonian edging pattern, it may not always be ideal for all lace patterns, and is not always the most successful method if placing beads on points for edgings, for example. The alternative is to use a crochet hook to place beads.

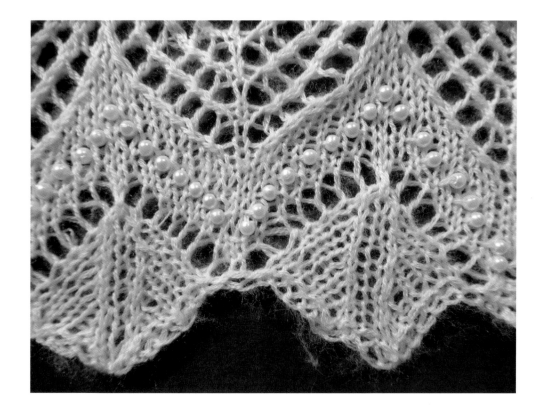

Estonian lace edge pattern with beads replacing nupps.

Placing a Bead Using the Crochet Hook Method
Choose a crochet hook which is fine enough to insert into the bead.

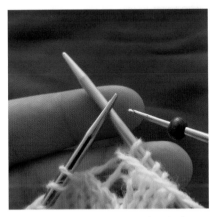

Knit to where the bead is to be placed. Place the bead onto the crochet hook.

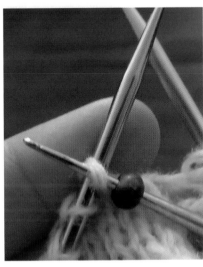

Use the crochet hook to pull the next stitch from the left-hand needle through the bead.

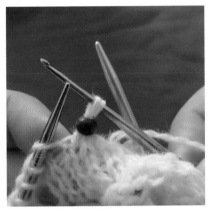

You may need to help by pushing the bead down to the base of the stitch.

Now return the stitch to the left-hand needle and work it in accordance with the pattern.

Now continue with your knitting to the next bead placement and repeat the process.

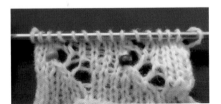

Placed beads.

The same process can be applied when knitting two stitches together where the bead needs to be placed on the decrease.

Demonstrations of both of these techniques can be easily found on YouTube if further assistance is required.

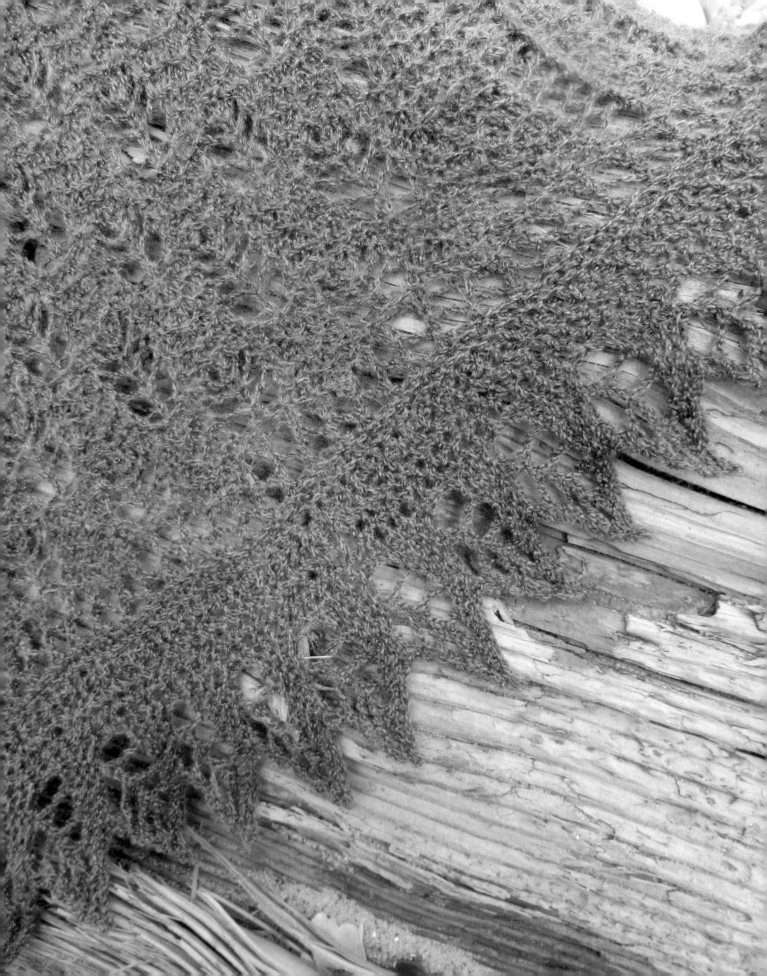

CHAPTER 6

PATTERN COMBINING AND MATERIALS

In this chapter we will start to put together some motifs, insertions and edgings. Using the Stitchionary, start thinking about what patterns and edgings might work well together. In order to demonstrate how this could work, we are going to look at combining motifs in order to knit a scarf or wrap. If there are motifs that you particularly like, try some swatches in your chosen yarn and block them and see what you think. Look at the options for introducing an insertion as a border down the sides. Does this work with the central pattern, and do you have an edging that you love and does it work with this particular combination? Repeat your swatch with both the border and the edging pattern. Does this produce a balanced pattern?

Try using a chart to see if your ideas will work together and to decide how to best place an edging to work and line up with your chosen all over pattern.

Try using your ideas to make a lacy scarf of your own design or if preferred, make the scarf to the Fir Cone design which is used to demonstrate this process. You could use the main design from this scarf but change the edges or the borders, it could be made wider or narrower than this design or even have some beads added or some sparkle.

However, if you want to replicate this scarf, then this is the information that will be needed. This scarf is made from a lace weight Cashmere Polyester blend. It is a very fluffy but very light yarn and beautifully soft, so it is ideal for a warm winter scarf, and the pattern shows up well following a good block.

Before you start, you will need to consider how your chosen yarn will react and what kind of fabric it will create when you knit it, thus swatching will be needed. This scarf was knitted on quite large needles to achieve an open pattern so that the fabric created would be light and airy and the pattern would show despite the halo created by the yarn. The pattern used in this example is the Fir Cone pattern which you can find in the Stitchionary. This is a garter stitch pattern which means that the scarf will have no wrong or right side. The scarf has a border of ladders up each side to provide a frame to the pattern and some structure to the fabric, which in this case it needed due to the very light and airy nature of the yarn. The scarf has a knitted-on border of Fern Leaves at the top and bottom. The shape of the Fern Leaf motif is similar to that of the Fir Cone pattern and consequently the two motifs are complimentary and work well together. The cast on is a provisional cast on, as described in the earlier section in this book. The scarf was deliberately made quite wide so that it would also be able to double as a warm pretty wrap, thus providing a more versatile finished item, than if it had been knitted purely as a scarf.

Hand drawn chart on squared paper.

Try out a swatch to see if the ideas worked together when knitted.

If, however, you would prefer to make a narrower version or a shorter version, you can do so. Calculating the desired width of the finished scarf can be done from the swatch once it has been fully blocked. You can then calculate how many pattern repeats – plus border – will be needed to achieve the desired dimensions. The pattern can be varied in a number of ways by leaving out one of the ladders from the borders, or indeed both if preferred. Choose another border pattern and add it onto the chart. Change the knitted-on edgings to your preferred option, ultimately producing a fully customized scarf or wrap, or combination entirely in line with your preferences, but try charting the design ideas before starting the knitting.

The chart and written instructions for this scarf can be found in the projects section towards the end of the book. These provide instructions for one pattern repeat of the central Fir Cone motif along with the side panels. Decide how many pattern repeats you want for your scarf, and then knit these repeats between the instructions for the ladder panels.

Including Lace in a Knitted Item or Garment

Why not revamp a favourite pattern with some lace? It is not difficult to pop in a lace border around the waist or bottom edge of a cardigan, for example, or a panel down the front of a sweater.

An otherwise rather plain grey sweater with the additional interest of an inserted central lace panel.

A pretty cardigan with an added lace edging.

A throw edged with a pretty lace edging.

Use a motif from the Stitchionary to make a pretty lacy cushion cover.

This is a sweater, improvised and knitted from the top down with the inclusion of a lace and cable panel down the front in order to create more interest to what would otherwise have been just a plain grey sweater.

In order to do this to vary a pattern, look at the calculations for the neck measurements on your sweater pattern. It will be necessary to swatch your panel, then block it and measure it. The panel will need to be placed either to the side if two panels were required or centrally as in this case. Calculate the placement of the panel so that it works with the neckline shaping of your pattern.

For example, this sweater, knitted from the top down, had a panel insertion of twenty-one stitches at the centre of the neck. It was therefore necessary to calculate at what point to insert the panel stitches in line with the graduating slope of the neck increases.

Using graph paper, it was plotted where the first purl stitch from the purl panels at either side of the motif should start on the front increase rows. Once this had been established, it was then possible to add in the next purl stitch on the panel on the next increase row before casting on the remaining stitches for the panel across the front and joining the sweater in the round. There should then be the required number of stitches on the needle for the neck line, and the shape has remained unaltered.

If knitting from the bottom up, the panel will need to be placed centrally above the welt. Once you reach the neckline the panel stitches can be plotted on graph paper to calculate the decreases. You could of course place panels at either side or both back and front, the choice is yours.

Why not replace the rib bands on a cardigan with a lace edging and transform an everyday cardigan into something special for a holiday or evening wear?

This cardigan is edged with Old Shell, knitted with the purl rows. The inclusion of the edging makes the cardigan just that bit more interesting and shows how easy it is to pop a lace edging onto a garment.

In order to do this, do not knit a rib at the bottom edge or around the sleeves. Either cast on as normal, and then pick up stitches around the bottom edge or use a provisional cast on so that the live stitches are easily available when the stage of knitting on the edging is reached. Once the cardigan is completed, using a long circular needle pick up stitches around the bottom edge, then pick up stitches in the usual way up the right front, across the back neck and down the left front. Count the stitches and make any adjustments that are needed to ensure that there are multiples of eighteen stitches. Place a marker and, working in the round, knit the Old Shell pattern for the desired width of the band. Cast off loosely. Knit a matching band at the edge of each sleeve.

There are any number of lace patterns that can be used to create beautiful all over patterns for sweaters and cardigans.

Lace can be added to almost anything. Why not incorporate lace into a cushion cover design, perhaps pairing it with the more frequently seen cable designs? Put a lace edging onto a throw or pretty blanket to give it a new feel.

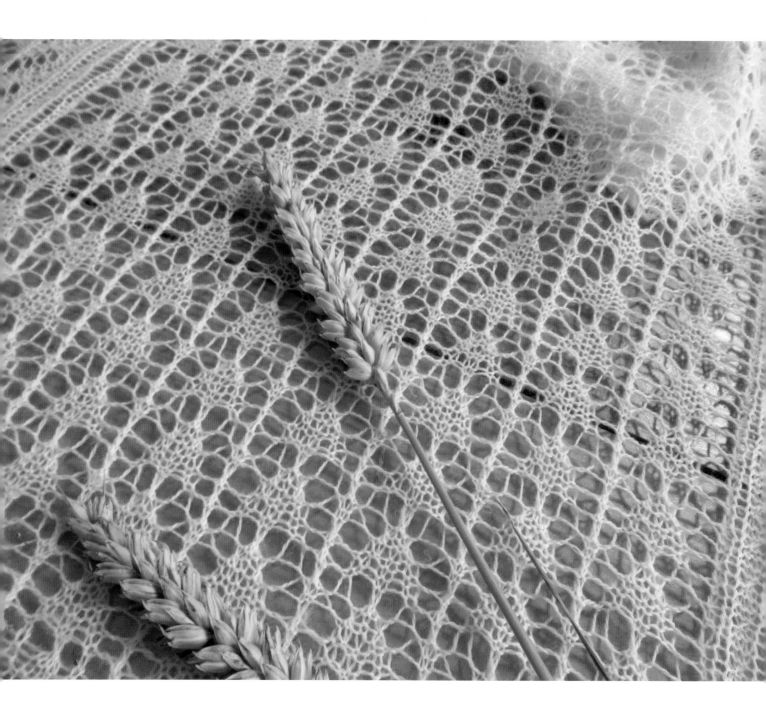

CHAPTER 7

FROM INSPIRATION TO STITCH

In this chapter, we will look at how to use inspirational material to design, plan and knit a beautiful but simple wrap. Both the examples that are being used here are wraps that have been designed for two separate weddings, using a slightly different approach in each case in order to illustrate how this can work.

So where does the inspiration for a pattern, a stitch or a motif come from? Lace motifs are invariably named for the things that people saw around them every day, so Falling Leaves, Twigs, Ploughed Acre, Paws, Shells and so forth. Estonian lace has motifs with names like Money and Wallpaper. It is worth noting that the names of the motifs, generally speaking, came after the pattern had been developed. This perhaps goes some way to explaining the variation in names for patterns even between neighbouring families, let alone different countries.

For the purposes of this book, we will be drawing on the lace motifs in the Stitchionary and will be using them to produce a beautiful and unique design. In order to help in the creation of this design, we will be looking at how to use inspiration from whatever sources we have available or are drawn to.

It is surprising how much of the world around us can be seen as knitting if things are looked at in a certain perspective. Look at the motifs in the Stitchionary and consider their names; for many of them the source of that inspiration is fairly immediately apparent. How often have you gone for a walk and seen flowers that look like stars, dewy cobwebs so reminiscent of delicate beaded lace, patterns in the sand, paw prints in the snow, snow

flakes, stars, frost patterns on leaves, and reflections in water? The list is almost endless.

But there is also inspiration to be found in man-made things as well. A set of lacy railings, mosaics and floor tiles can all provide a starting point for a lace design. Magnified images of cell structures can provide quite breath-taking lacy images that will have you reaching for your knitting needles. You never know when you might see something that will spark an idea so it is a good idea to try to have some means of recording these when you spot them. For most us in this day and age, that is most likely to be the camera on our phone, but pencil on the back of an envelope also works.

Once having captured your inspirational images, the challenge is then to take them forward to a piece of knitting. Probably the easiest way to explain some of the ways that this process can work is by following the design journey and construction of two different wedding wraps. In both cases the brief was for a simple but beautiful shawl appropriate for a rustic country summer wedding.

The first of these designs was to provide bridesmaids' shawls that would both be in keeping with the theme of the wedding, but would also provide some warmth for later in the evening, or in the event that the weather on the day was cooler than hoped.

The commission was from the bride who had clear ideas about what she wanted. To start the process, I collected fabric scraps from the bridesmaids' dresses, which included lace trims

Snow creates a bead pattern on winter grasses.

A delicate dandelion clock could be the starting idea for a round, centre out shawl.

This starry plant is reminiscent of Estonian Star stitch.

Summer flowers suggest starting points for lacy designs.

Alpaca wrap in Vertical Trellis Faggot stitch is the starting point for this project.

Mood board exploration.

Exploring shapes and textures.

and explored the style of the dresses and the texture and colours of the fabrics. I combined this with images of the proposed flowers and then brainstormed associated and linked images on a series of mood boards. The bride's initial thoughts revolved around a Faggot stitch scarf that she liked in quite a heavy weight yarn, because of its simplicity, and the initial exploration for the ultimate design of the wedding wraps started with that first image.

It was evident that, in order to capture the mood of the wedding, this would need to be a light and airy wrap, and with a more delicate pattern than the Faggot stitch wrap, so both the type and the colour of the yarn that was to be used were important. For the summer, pure cashmere, although a luxurious fibre and thus appropriate for the occasion seemed

too warm, a traditional Shetland cobweb weight yarn which would have had excellent stitch definition and really suited the pattern, was also felt to be too warm and potentially an issue with skin sensitivity for at least one of the bridesmaids. Therefore a blend of cashmere with a fine cotton was experimented with and proved to have good stitch definition and a beautiful soft, light and airy fabric with lovely drape but less memory than a traditional Shetland yarn.

The colour ultimately chosen was a natural white, as opposed to the undyed creamier colour of the yarn, another option which was explored but looked tired against the blues and greys of the bridesmaids' dresses.

The flower shapes from the mood boards became increasingly dominant, daisy, cornflower and the romantically named

A natural white worked better with the colours than undyed yarn.

Flower shapes became increasingly important.

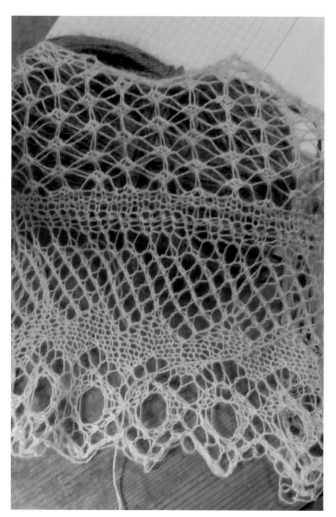

An early sampling of Bead lace with an Irish lace border.

'Love in a Mist', all leading to an exploration of star shaped lace. Whilst Estonian Star Flower stitch was a contender it seemed a bit overwhelming for the brief and potentially in competition with the lace on the dresses. However, the simpler and airier Shetland Bead lace appeared to lend itself perfectly to this image and still complemented the slightly spiked starry effect from the flowers, whilst retaining some relationship with the original Faggot stitch scarf.

The requirement that the wrap should not be too fancy meant that there were no side borders other than a plain garter stitch band. The final decision for an edging at either end incorporates a band of Faggot stitch as part of a traditional Irish lace edging which is knitted on after the wrap has been completed. This gave reference to the initial image of the Faggot stitch wrap where this journey had begun, whilst the larger holes in the edging continue to emulate the flower shapes of the main wrap. In addition, the edging was not 'too pointy', another specific requirement in the brief.

Bead lace and edging showing how light and airy the finished wraps were.

The pattern and charts for this wrap are included in Chapter 9 – Projects, later in this book. These can be knitted as written, but you should swatch and block with your chosen yarn first.

If new to lace knitting, it would be helpful to practise this stitch before embarking on the project. Although the pattern is only a four row and six stitch repeat, it is two-sided lace, which means that there are no rest rows, and it is a pattern that does require some concentration to keep track of the stitches.

A side border could be a good addition to this wrap. Look at the Stitchionary and experiment with some of the border patterns to see what would work. Does the border need to include a line of ladders or lace holes between it and the centre pattern? Try charting some ideas on some squared paper and knit up some swatches to see how they look. It may be that edgings need to be changed as the ones in the pattern may not work so well with the chosen border pattern.

Explore the options, think about what might work, swatch a mini wrap with both border and edging, and block and then leave it for a few hours or until the following day. Come back and look at it again – does it work, is it as attractive as you thought it was when you first looked at it? Have you got the needle size right? As a fabric does it have the drape and stitch

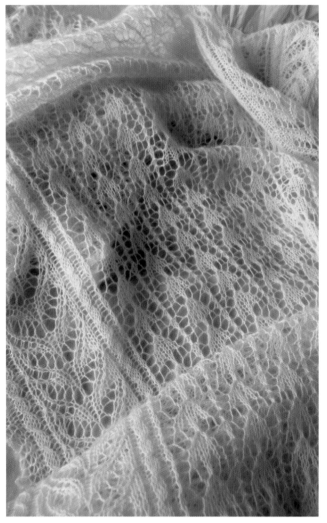

Harebell lace wedding wrap.

definition that you were aiming for? If the answer is no, then what is it that does not work? Maybe this is not the best stitch pattern for your chosen yarn, maybe it is knitted too tight or too loose, or the motifs that you have put together just do not go together well. Once you have worked out what the issue is then you can confidently swatch again, wiser in light of your previous experience.

The beauty of this pattern is that you can cast on as many stitches as you want so long as you keep the multiples correct for the stitch pattern and consequently, you can vary the width, making it as wide or as narrow as you wish. It is a pattern that you can knit until you think the wrap is long enough; it is not necessary to calculate the finished length before you begin unless you wish to do so. Do remember that once it is blocked it will grow, both in width and length. Additionally, the pattern does not have a right or wrong side, nor a right way or wrong way up, which would necessitate knitting the wrap in two halves and then grafting the two sections together – something which clearly creates an additional complication both in the planning process but also in the execution of the graft of the lace itself.

It may be helpful to know that if you use a yarn as fine as the lace weight yarn used in the original pattern, which was an NM 2/33, a fine lace weight yarn, then to produce a wrap of similar proportions to mine, you will need at least thirty-eight grams. And yes, it can be pulled through a wedding ring!

The second wrap was designed for a bride, again for a summer wedding and it was to be a surprise. In order to gather some ideas, I was able to obtain some information about the style of the wedding. It was to be a relaxed event at a beautiful country house, with the evening event in a large tepee.

For this shawl, I was not able to use information about the bride's dress or the bridesmaids' dresses as these were secret. However, I did know that the flowers were going to be country cottage style and that the wedding cake was a naked cake with edible flowers. I was able to use this and information about the bride herself and her life to help inspire the design.

The completed wrap. If you look carefully you may be able to see where the Harebells change direction at the mid-point graft.

The central motif is Harebell or Snowdrop lace. This both related to the country setting of the wedding, the choice of flowers for the event, and also reflected the childhood home of the bride who had lived in the country in an area where flowers were produced for the flower markets. The little cable ropes down the sides of the wrap are a reflection of the bride's degree in knitwear and design, and relate to her final collection before graduating. The chevrons in the border are almost heart shaped, but not enough to appear too sentimental. The peaks in the edging at the bottom reflect the snowy alpine mountains as the bride and groom met whilst both were working in the winter ski resorts. The whole thing then comes together to provide a special shawl with a very personal legend for the bride.

This shawl is very long as the bride was particularly tall.

However, yours can be any length that is right for you. It should be noted, however, that the shawl is knitted in two halves and then grafted together in the middle. The edges are knitted on after the centre has been worked.

Again, this shawl can be knitted according to the pattern, or it can be easily varied, perhaps by changing the side panels, or using a different edging.

If you are new to lace knitting you will find the Harebell pattern less challenging than the Bead pattern in the previous wrap as it is only patterned on the right side rows. The borders might feel slightly more challenging. If you knit a swatch before beginning, it will be easier to see how the different sections fit together. Use stitch markers to show where the different sections start and finish and to help you keep track of your stitches.

CHAPTER 8

FINISHING TECHNIQUES

For a lot of people the finishing of a project can feel like a chore. Nevertheless, it is as important as the process of creating the project and it is worth taking time to complete the finishing process properly in order to set off your hard work. No matter how hard you try there will always be ends to sew in.

With all knitting, but especially with lace, if one of the yarn joins mentioned in Chapter 3 – Techniques is not an option, it is always best to try to ensure that any new yarn is introduced at the beginning of a row. This makes it easy to sew ends in along the edge, thus making them as invisible as possible. If knitting using round needles then consider where is likely to be the best place to introduce a fresh ball of yarn or new colour. If it is necessary to have a join mid row, then aiming to place any join on a decrease will allow the join to disappear into the texture of the decrease itself and should render it more or less invisible.

When leaving ends to be sewn in, it is important to leave long enough tails so that they can be securely darned in. To sew in your ends you will need a blunt ended needle or a wool needle.

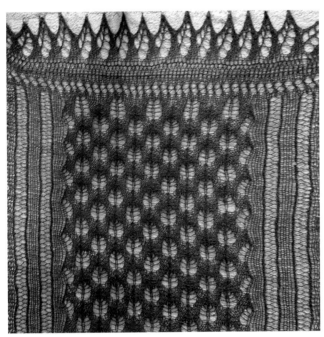

Fir Cone scarf pinned out for blocking. This shows how the lace opens up when stretched.

Think about the direction you should take the yarn in order to ensure that there are no holes on the right side. Carefully weave the yarn in, making sure not to pucker or distort the fabric. It is a good idea to give the knitting a good stretch at this point. With lace, it is advisable to wash and block before finally cutting the yarn. This ensures that the ends will not come undone whilst the lace is being blocked.

Cut the ends carefully with small sharp scissors to ensure that you do not snag your lace.

Grafting, which is also known as Kitchener stitch, is a technique used to join knitting invisibly by using a sewing needle to join live stitches at a point where a seam might otherwise be placed. Kitchener stitch allows you in effect to knit the two seams together. This is especially useful if you have a pattern with a distinct right way up, that needs to be joined in the middle, something not uncommon in lace knitting.

If grafting lace, try to choose a row that has a minimum of yarn overs. Wherever possible, graft on a wrong side row with minimal or no patterning.

There is a lot of advice about how to graft and to some extent, how you go about it is a matter for you and will be as a result of trial and error. It is definitely worth practising this technique, and although it may seem challenging the finished results are well worth the effort.

Some knitters advocate removing your stitches from the needles prior to grafting. Whilst this may be effective with thicker and sticky yarns or in projects that do not involve lace, you may find that it is far less risky to remove the stitches as you graft. Pay attention to your tension as you graft, it should be consistent with the knitting. If you pull it too tight you will be left with a ridge.

For those less familiar with using Kitchener stitch, you might find it helpful to track down a live demonstration on YouTube.

Grafting on Stocking Stitch

Ensure that each needle has a long tail of yarn sufficient for the graft or use a length of matching yarn. Arrange your needles so that they are side by side with the right sides uppermost. Thread the yarn from the back needle onto a blunt ended wool or darning needle.

Step 1   Insert the wool needle purlwise into the first stitch on the front needle, draw the yarn through and leave the stitch on the needle.

Step 2   Now bring the yarn knitwise through the first stitch on the back needle. Draw the yarn through and leave the stitch on the needle.

Step 3   *Bring the yarn through the first stitch on the front needle knitwise and slip this stitch off the needle.

Step 4   Bring the yarn through the next stitch on the front needle purlwise, then leave this stitch on the needle.

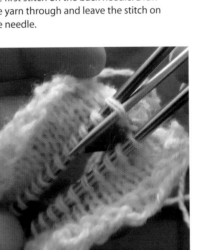

Step 5   Bring the yarn through the first stitch on the back needle purlwise and slip this stitch off the needle.

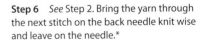

Step 6   *See* Step 2. Bring the yarn through the next stitch on the back needle knit wise and leave on the needle.*

Repeat steps three through to six between the asterisks until one stitch remains on each needle.

Bring the yarn through the stitch on the front needle knitwise and slip the stitch off.

Bring the yarn through the stitch on the back needle purlwise and slip the stitch off.

Check your tension and fasten off any loose ends.

Grafting on Garter Stitch

Arrange your knitting so that the front needle has the bumps and the back needle has the smooth purl stitches.

Step 1 Now with your sewing needle threaded with yarn, bring the yarn through the first stitch on the front needle purlwise and leave this stitch on the needle.

Step 2 Take the yarn through the first stitch on the back needle purlwise and leave it on the needle.

Step 3 *Bring the yarn through the first stitch on the front needle knitwise and slip this stitch off the needle.

Step 4 Bring the yarn through the next stitch on the front needle purlwise and leave the stitch on the needle.

Step 5 Bring the yarn through the first stitch on the back needle knitwise and slip the stitch off the needle.

Step 6 As with step 2, take the yarn through the next stitch on the back needle purlwise and leave on the needle.*

Repeat steps three through to six, between the asterisks until one stitch remains on each needle.

Bring the yarn through the last stitch on the front needle knitwise and slip off the needle.

Bring the yarn through the last stitch on the back needle knitwise and slip off the needle.

Check your tension. Fasten off loose ends.

Washing and Blocking

Earlier in the book we looked at using coned yarns bought from the mills and it was pointed out that these yarns need special treatment to remove the lubricants that are applied to them to enable them to be used with commercial knitting machines.

It is not a difficult thing to do but is obviously one more task to complete before your knitted piece can be appreciated in all its glory! These lubricants, often referred to as oils, need to be removed either before or after knitting. In order to do this, follow these steps.

Step 1

Take your knitted swatch and immerse it in the hottest water you can put your hands into. (Yes, really!) Add some washing up soap; do not agitate the yarn but just leave to soak.

In all probability, you will see that the water looks quite dirty or cloudy as the lubricants leach out of the yarn. This applies to any yarn that contains machine oils, and whilst the idea of treating your beautiful Cashmere or other fine and delicate yarns in such an apparently brutal manner may seem appalling, it does not damage the yarn and the end result is beautiful, soft, gorgeous fibre.

Step 2

Next rinse your swatch, again with very hot water until the water runs clear.

Occasionally some yarn may need two immersions in very hot water and washing up soap before the oils are fully removed.

Step 3

Now roll your swatch in a towel to remove the excess water, then pin out to block and allow to dry.

Once dry, measure the swatch, calculate the stitch gauge and use this to inform your approach to the design that you have in mind.

Knitted swatches being cleaned in very hot water with soap.

The process for cleaning your finished project is the same as for the swatch. Whilst it sounds counterintuitive to suggest treating a precious piece of knitting, or a luxury high end yarn in such a callous way, the transformation that occurs during the washing process is nothing short of magical, turning stringy uninspiring looking yarn into something soft, squidgy and beautiful. Additionally, you have the reassurance of having already treated your swatch in the same manner so you will know what the impact of this treatment will be on the finished piece of knitting.

For yarn that has been produced for the hand knitter and that therefore does not need the specialist cleaning as described above for the coned yarns, the process for blocking is more straightforward.

Once you have finished knitting, you will still need to wash the lace before blocking. This will transform what may well appear to be a not particularly inspiring piece of knitting at this point.

Follow the wash care instructions as indicated on the ball band and carefully wash the lace in warm water. Consider using one of the wool soak products that are now widely available which reduce the need for agitation and rinsing, and which gently re-condition your yarn. Gently squeeze out excess water, and then roll in a towel.

Fir Cone scarf pulled out, with wires threaded and then pinned onto a towel-covered mat. Note the wires are only threaded through the peaks on the Fern lace edging.

Take your still wet lace, and stretch it out on the blocking boards, pinning it and then leaving to dry.

This process is much improved by the use of blocking wires which are inserted along the straight edges of your lace and through the peaks on edgings. The wires are then pinned to the board with T pins. This method makes the process of ensuring that your lace is blocked correctly much easier and the finished result tends to be better than if you simply pin the lace.

Blocking wires are readily available to buy and come in a variety of lengths.

Blocking boards are also readily available to buy; however, using the large grey rubber tiles sold for garage or workshop flooring works just as well and they are somewhat cheaper. As with blocking boards, these can be joined together like a jigsaw, in different ways to cater for the size and shape of knitted lace. They are very sturdy and provide a firm base for your blocking. T pins work quite happily with these boards but you can also use mapping pins to secure the wires if you run out of T pins. These provide an equally secure hold on your blocking wires.

Block with care; you will already have blocked your swatch so you will have some idea of how far you can safely stretch out your lace for optimal effect. You should be aware that some yarns are not as strong as others, and that wet wool is not as strong, and that consequently for some yarns, very severe blocking could result in breakages.

Thread the blocking wires through the loops along the straight edges of your wet lace, and through the peaks only of edging stitches. Then, using pins, carefully pull out and secure your lace. The lace should be left to dry. It can then be unpinned, any ends snipped off, and you can finally sit back and admire your beautiful piece of knitted lace.

If you do not own blocking boards, it is entirely possible to block onto towels, bed spreads, mattresses, or even a carpet. Anywhere in fact that will provide a secure hold for your pinned lace.

You may well be familiar with the traditional blocking frames or stretchers used by the Shetland knitters, often seen in great profusion in historic pictures. These provide the optimal blocking experience, and have the great advantage that they do not take up very much room and can be leant against a wall or propped up outside on a nice day. They are not particularly easy to acquire. If you search on the internet, you can find instructions for making your own blocking frames.

This is a miniature Hap stretcher photographed at the Lerwick Textile Museum. It demonstrates the way in which these are used to stretch the lace and the way in which only the points are threaded.

After Care and International Wash Care Instructions

If you want your beautiful lace and all your hard work to last, then after care and correct washing are important.

If you have made your item from yarn that has been produced for the hand knitter then it will have come with a ball band, which amongst other things contains the information needed to both wash and press your item. These instructions should be followed. It is also helpful to save the ball band for future reference.

If you have used coned yarn from the mills and removed the machine oils, as described earlier, then your future washing and general care of your knitted item will be the same or very similar to that of other knitted fabrics. That is to say that they should be washed very carefully by hand in warm water. The excess water should be removed by very gentle squeezing and by then rolling in a towel before pinning out to dry. Occasionally these mill end yarns will indicate that they are 'super wash', meaning that they can be washed at the appropriate wool care setting in a washing machine. The exercise of some caution is advised

in this regard, and before subjecting your hard work and skill to the vagaries of the washing machine, it would be sensible to wash the swatch in the machine first and see what happens.

When it comes to ironing, steaming and pressing, it is best not to place the iron directly onto your knitted item, as to do so flattens the stitches and can effectively ruin the texture of your knitting. To steam with a steam iron, hold the iron a few centimetres above the knitting, and let the steam permeate the knitting. Some irons have an option to blast additional steam through the fabric if needed.

If a steam iron is not available, then the traditional method of steaming, using a damp cloth placed over the knitting with very gentle pressure from the iron, will also work, although holding the iron just above the damp cloth and using the heat from the iron to push the steam through the knitted fabric reduces the risk of inadvertently flattening out the stitches whilst they are hidden from view.

When knitted lace needs to be washed, it may be in some cases that it will need to be re-blocked although not so vigorously. On the whole, it may well be that providing you stretch your lace out on a flat surface on a towel and pull out any peaks on the edging, this will be sufficient. If, however, it is necessary to completely re-block your lace then follow the instructions above and repeat the process of blocking that you undertook when you first finished the item.

The information below provides guidance on the most commonly used care symbols for wool and yarn.

Laundry Care Symbols

	Very gentle wash, number denotes maximum temperature
	Do not tumble dry
	Hand wash only
	Do not dry clean
	Do not iron
	Dry flat
	Steam
	Iron, low heat
	Iron, medium heat.

CHAPTER 9

PROJECTS

Razor Shell Socks

These socks are knitted in a lace weight Alpaca but with three ends held together resulting in a 4 ply/fingering weight yarn. They are the warm soft kind of socks that you want to be wearing in front of a lovely fire or snuggled up in bed on a cold winter night!

Their construction is very straightforward and the Razor Shell pattern is a simple one to complete and very effective, and like so many lace patterns, it looks more complex than it actually is. These socks do not have a rib cuff as the Razor Shell pattern produces an attractive fluted edge. If you want to use them as day socks then you can of course add a ribbed cuff before starting to work the pattern.

Razor Shell socks.

You will observe that this version of Razor Shell is worked on a stocking stitch ground, thus all rounds are knitted.

The pattern is worked in multiples of six stitches.

- Gauge: Using 3mm double pointed needles or size needed to obtain gauge measured over the pattern; 30 stitches × 40 rows to 10cm.
- For foot sizes small (medium, large).

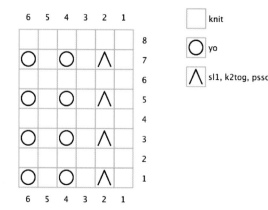

Chart for Razor Shell sock pattern.

Cast on 54 (60,66) stitches. Divide the stitches between 3 dpn needles as follows: Needle 1,18 (18,18) stitches, needle 2,18 (18,24) stitches and needle 3,18 (24,24) stitches and then join in the round. You will have multiples of the lace pattern on each needle.

Round 1: knit

Round 2: start chart or round 1 of the written lace pattern.

Razor Shell Socks Lace Instructions

Round 1 and all odd-numbered rounds: K, sl1, k2tog, psso, (k, yo) × 2.

Round 2 and all even-numbered rounds: Knit (6 sts).

Continue working the lace pattern until the sock cuff is the length you require.

Divide for heel at the end of a knit round on needle 3. K 4(3,3) sts from N1 onto N3. Then move 4(3,3) sts from needle 2 to the other end of needle 3. N3 should now have 26(30,30) stitches. Place the remaining stitches on N1 and N2 onto one needle which should now have 28(30,36) stitches.

Start the heel.

Slip the first stitch of every row and work over the heel sts in stocking stitch until heel flap measures 6.5cm or desired length.

With RS facing:

Row 1: Slip the first stitch, knit 14(16,16) k2tog tbl, knit 1, turn.

Row 2: Slip 1, purl 5(5, 5) sts, purl 2 tog, purl 1, turn.

Row 3: Slip 1, knit to 1 stitch before the gap and knit this stitch together with next stitch tbl as before, knit 1, turn.

Row 4: Slip 1, purl to 1 stitch before gap, purl this stitch together with next stitch as before, purl 1, turn.

Repeat rows 3 and 4 until all stitches have been worked, ending on a WS row. 16(18,18) sts.

With RS facing, knit across all stitches on needle.

Now pick up and knit 13(16,16) stitches down the side of the heel flap and add them to them to your current working needle which becomes N1. You will now have 29(34,34) sts on needle 1. Work across the sts on the next needle (needle 2), keeping the pattern as set. With a new needle N3, pick up and knit 13(16,16) sts along left gusset, then knit 8(9,9) from needle 1.

N1 will now have 21(25,25) sts.

N3 will have 21(25,25) sts.

Rnd 1: N1, k to last 3 stitches, k 2tog, k1.

Rnd 1: N2, k across pattern stitches as set.

Rnd 1: N3, k1, ssk, k to end.

Rnd 2: knit all stitches on needles 1 and 3 and pattern across needle 2.

Repeat rounds 1 and 2 until 13(15, 15) stitches remain on needle 1 and 3.

Continue to knit all stitches on needles 1 and 3 and to pattern across the stitches on needle 2 until your sock is 5cm less than the desired length before working toe decreases. Note the lace pattern stops once toe decreases start.

Now decrease for the toe as follows:

Rnd 1: N1, knit to last 3 stitches, k2tog, k1

N2, k1, ssk, k across to last 3 stitches, k2tog, k1

N3, k1, ssk, knit to end.

Rnd 2–4: knit.

Rnd 5: as rnd 1.

Rnd 6–7: knit.

Rnd 8: as round 1.

Rnd 9–10: knit.

Rnd 11: as round 1.

Rnd 12: knit.

Rnd 13: as round 1.

Rnd 14: knit.

Rnd 15: as round 1.

Rnd 16: knit.

Thereafter repeat round 1 until 12 stitches remain.

Graft the remaining stitches using Kitchener stitch.

Make the second sock to match the first.

Sew in ends, wash and block.

Finished Razor Shell socks.

Fir Cone Scarf

This scarf is knitted in a lace weight Cashmere blend. The Pine Cone pattern is on a garter stitch base and therefore has no right or wrong side. It is a wide scarf so it could also be used as an elegant wrap if wished. If you prefer a narrower scarf then reduce the number of pattern repeats, and cast on fewer stitches.

The borders are simple ladders, but you could replace these with an alternative panel if you wish.

The edging is Fern Lace edging (sometimes called Oak Leaf edging). The little fern leaves pick up on the pattern of the pine cones. This provides a pleasing similarity in terms of pattern matching for this scarf. An alternative edging can be chosen if wished, just remember to think about how the patterns will work together before finally committing. As ever try a swatch first with the chosen edging knitted onto the fir cone design.

Fir Cone scarf.

Instructions for Knitting

To knit this scarf, cast on multiples of ten stitches for the Fir Cone pattern, plus eleven side stitches, twenty-four stitches for the ladders, and six stitches for the garter edges. Based on the swatch, you will know how wide the scarf will be so you will be able to calculate the amount of stitches accordingly.

Cast on your required number of stitches using a provisional cast on.

Knit 4 rows in garter stitch.

With RS facing, begin the Fir Cone chart, and repeat this until your scarf is the desired length, ending on a wrong side row.

With RS facing knit 4 rows in garter stitch.

Next Row RS: K1, (yo, k2tog) to end.
Next Row WS: knit.
Next Row RS: sl1, k1, psso, yo, repeat to end, k1.
Next Row WS: knit.

With the RS facing, knit across the following row to the end.

Turn work and using the lace cast on, cast on 10 sts. These are your stitches for the knitted-on edging.

With WS facing, knit the first 9 of your cast on stitches, then knit the 10th stitch together with the first stitch on the left-hand needle from the scarf. Do this on every WS row.

Turn the work, RS facing, slip the first stitch, then continue with Row 1 of the Fern Leaf edging chart.

For the Fern Leaf edging that is used in this pattern please go to the Stitchionary in Chapter 4 where the chart and written instructions for this edging will be found. Other possible options can also be considered by a perusal of the other edgings contained in this section of the book.

Once you have decided on your edging motif, repeat the chart pattern, knitting the last stitch from the edging together with the first stitch from the scarf on each wrong side row and slipping the first stitch on the right side until all the stitches have been worked.

On the last wrong side row, there should be 1 stitch remaining from the scarf pattern. With the wrong side facing, cast off in the normal way. When you get to the last edging stitch, knit it together with the remaining stitch from the scarf, then cast off the last 2 stitches in the normal manner and fasten off.

To knit on the second edging, carefully unpick the provisional cast on and pick up the live stitches.

Complete the second edging as above, omitting the garter stitch rows which you completed at the beginning of the scarf, therefore you are starting with the 4 rows of Faggot stitch.

To finish, carefully sew in any loose ends, then wet block to pull out the lace.

Fir Cone Scarf Written Instruction

Row 1 (RS): Sl, (k4, yo, ssk) × 2, k3, yo, k3, sl1, k2tog, psso, k3, yo, k1, yo, k3, sl1, k2tog, psso, k3, yo, k5, yo, ssk, k4, yo, ssk, k3. (51 sts)

Row 2 and all WS rows: Sl wyif, (p4, yo, p2tog) × 2, p27, yo, p2tog, p4, yo, p2tog, p3.

Row 3: Repeat row 1.

Row 5: Repeat row 1.

Row 7: Repeat row 1.

Row 9: Sl, (k4, yo, ssk) × 2, k2, k2tog, k3, yo, k1, yo, k3, sl1, k2tog, psso, k3, yo, k1, yo, k3, (ssk, k4, yo) × 2, ssk, k3.

Row 11: Repeat row 9.

Row 13: Repeat row 9.

Row 15: Repeat row 9.

knit

V slip

O yo

\ ssk

/ k2tog

Λ sl1, k2tog, psso

Edge stitches

10 Stitch repeat

highlight for multiple dec

Fir Cone scarf main pattern chart.

Alpaca scarf.

Alpaca Scarf

This Alpaca scarf, which is wide enough to use as a wrap, was the original inspiration for the bead lace wedding shawls featured earlier in this book.

This is a very simple pattern that uses Vertical Trellis Faggoting throughout with simple garter borders. The pattern demonstrates that some of the simplest patterns when used on their own can create very attractive results. You could add a border to this design, perhaps lace ladders or lace holes, for example.

This scarf can be knitted in any weight of wool, and made with any width and any length. Although alternate rows are purl rows because of the way that the pattern works, there is no obvious right or wrong side. This Alpaca scarf was knitted with a fingering weight yarn and produced a really warm and versatile scarf.

Think about the kind of fabric you would like to create. Do you want a super warm but still airy scarf, or something lighter that would work as a wrap on a summer holiday? Select your yarn, swatch and block a sample then cast on and knit!

Remember, this pattern is worked on an odd number of stitches. The chart and written instructions for this stitch pattern can be found in Chapter 4 – Stitchionary.

Once the work is to you desired length, cast off all stitches. Sew in any loose ends, wash and block.

Bridesmaids wearing bead lace shawls.

Bridesmaid's Shawl: Bead Lace

Knitted in a fine lace weight cotton Cashmere yarn.

- You will need approximately 38grms or 560m of 2/33 nm or very fine lace weight yarn to complete a shawl.
- Tension after blocking: with 3mm needles 43 sts to 7.5 inches over bead pattern.
- Finished blocked size is approximately 170cm × 50cm.
- The edging is knitted on after completion of centre panel.
- Skills required: mastery of basic knitted lace and ability to read charts.

Bridesmaid's shawl detail.

Instructions for Knitting

With 3.00mm needles using a provisional cast on (*see* note below) cast on 103 stitches.

Knit six rows in garter stitch.

The first stitch of every row is slipped.

The first three stitches and the last three stitches of every row are knitted.

With right side (RS) facing, begin chart A, bead pattern. Complete 94 repeats ending on row 4, with right side facing.

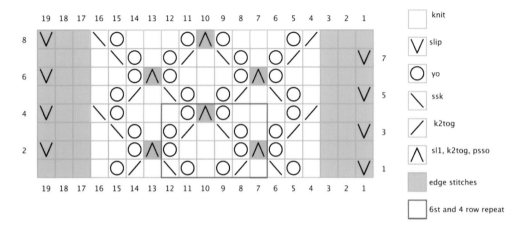

Bead lace pattern chart.

Bead Lace Bridesmaid's Shawl Instructions

Row 1 (RS): Sl, k3, yo, ssk, k, k2tog, yo, k, yo, ssk, k, k2tog, yo, k4 (19 sts).

Row 2 (WS): Sl, k4, yo, sl, k2tog, psso, yo, k3, yo, sl, k2tog, psso, yo, k5.

Row 3: Sl, k3, k2tog, yo, k, yo, ssk, k, k2tog, yo, k, yo, ssk, k4.

Row 4: Sl, k2, ssk, yo, k3, yo, sl, k2tog, psso, yo, k3, yo, k2tog, k3.

Rows 5–8: Repeat rows 1–4.

Knit 7 rows, ending with a RS row.

Turn to the chart and written instructions for the Irish Lace edging, which can be found in the edgings section of Chapter 4 – Stitchionary.

WS is now facing, cast on 20 sts and starting with row 12 of the Irish Lace edging, k to last st on right-hand needle and knit it together with the first stitch on the left-hand needle. Do this at the end of every even row.

Turn work and follow chart until all stitches but 1 have been knitted from the LH needle.

With WS facing and using a lace cast off, cast off all stitches until 2 remain on LH needle and one remains on RH needle. Knit the last stitch on RH needle together with remaining stitch on left hand needle, 2 sts remaining, cast off last 2 sts.

Carefully unravel the provisional cast on and pick up the stitches (103). With RS facing, knit across all sts. Turn the work and WS facing, cast on 20 sts. Proceed as above until all stitches have been worked.

Sew in ends. Soak in warm water, then wet block to size. Leave to dry.

Special Instructions

Provisional cast on: using waste yarn cast on the required number of stitches, knit 2 rows in waste yarn. Join in main yarn, and knit across all stitches, this is now the right side. Complete pattern.

To knit on the edging, carefully unpick the stitches from the waste yarn and place the live stitches on the needle. Then follow pattern as written.

Completed bridesmaid's shawl.

The bride wearing her Harebell Lace wrap.

Bride's Wrap: Harebell Lace

Knitted in a fine lace weight extra fine Merino yarn.

- You will need approximately 100grms of 2/30 nm or fine lace weight yarn to complete a shawl.
- Tension after blocking: with 3mm needles 16 sts to 7.5cm over Harebell pattern.
- The edging is knitted on after completion of centre panel.
- Skills required: mastery of basic knitted lace and ability to read charts.

Bride's wrap.

Instructions for Knitting

With 3.00mm needles using a provisional cast on (*see* note below), cast on 112 sts (7 pattern repeats of Harebell pattern plus 6 edge stitches + chevron and cable borders, 25 sts each).

You may find it helpful to place markers at the beginning and end of the Harebell pattern, at least until the pattern is set.

Knit 6 rows in garter st.

With right side (RS) facing begin chart A, Harebell and border pattern. Complete as many times as required to obtain half the length ending on an 8th row with right side facing.

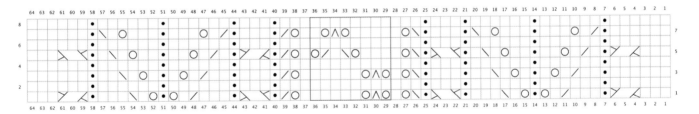

Chart for main pattern of Harebell lace wrap.

Harebell Lace Bride's Wrap Instructions

Row 1 (RS): K3, 2/1 RC, p, k3, k2tog, k, yo, p, yo, k, ssk, k3, p, 2/1 LC, p, ssk, yo, k, yo, sl1, k2tog, psso, yo, k6, yo, k2tog, p, 2/1 LC, p, k3, k2tog, k, yo, p, yo, k, ssk, k3, p, 2/1 RC, k3 (64 sts).

Row 2 and all WS rows: (P6, k) × 3, p3, k, p14, k, p3, (k, p6) × 3.

Row 3: K6, p, k2, k2tog, k, yo, k, p, k, yo, k, ssk, k2, p, k3, p, ssk, yo, k, yo, sl1, k2tog, psso, yo, k6, yo, k2tog, p, k3, p, k2, k2tog, k, yo, k, p, k, yo, k, ssk, k2, p, k6.

Row 5: K3, 2/1 RC, p, k, k2tog, k, yo, k2, p, k2, yo, k, ssk, k, p, 2/1 LC, p, ssk, yo, k4, yo, ssk, k, k2tog, yo, k, yo, k2tog, p, 2/1 RC, p, k, k2tog, k, yo, k2, p, k2, yo, k, ssk, k, p, 2/1 LC, k3.

Row 7: K6, p, k2tog, k, yo, k3, p, k3, yo, k, ssk, p, k3, p, ssk, yo, k5, yo, sl1, k2tog, psso, yo, k2, yo, k2tog, p, k3, p, k2tog, k, yo, k3, p, k3, yo, k, ssk, p, k6.

Now set aside the first half, and cast on a further 112 sts and complete the pattern to match the first half.

Graft the 2 sections together in the middle, following the instructions for grafting set out in Chapter 8 – Finishing Techniques. Note that there will be both stocking stitch and garter stitches to graft. Keep an eye on the tension to ensure that a ridge is not created.

Next, turn to the chart and written instructions for the wave edging, Chapter 4 – Stitchionary in the section containing edgings.

Now unpick the stitches from the provisional cast on and place them on your needle.

Knit across the row ending with the WS facing.

Cast on 12 sts and starting with row 14 of the chart for Wave Edging k to last st on rt hand needle and knit it together with first stitch on left hand needle. Do this at the end of every even row.

Turn work and follow chart until all stitches but 1 have been knitted.

With WS facing and using a lace cast off, cast off all stitches until 2 remain on LH needle and one remains on RH needle. Knit the last stitch on rt hand needle together with remaining stitch on left hand needle, 2 sts remaining, cast off last 2 sts.

Carefully unravel the provisional cast on from the other end of the wrap and pick up the stitches.

With RS facing knit across all sts. Turn the work and with WS facing Cast on 20 sts. Proceed as above until all stitches have been worked.

Sew in ends. Soak in warm water, then wet block to size. Leave to dry.

Special Note

Provisional cast on: using waste yarn, cast on the required number of stitches, knit two rows in waste yarn. Join in main yarn, and knit across all stitches, this is now the right side. Complete pattern.

To knit on the edging, carefully unpick the stitches from the waste yarn and place the live stitches on the needle. Then follow pattern as written.

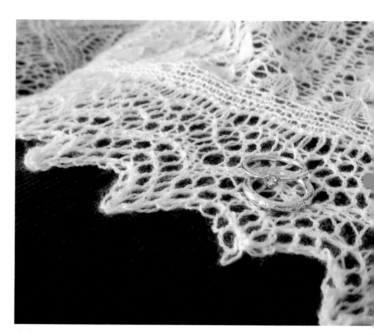

Harebell lace wrap showing Wave edging.

Hap Throw

This throw is based on the traditional Haps worn by the working women of Shetland in days gone by. These shawls feature frequently in old photographs of the women as they went about their daily tasks, knitting as they went. This pattern is not designed to be a shawl although, as it is made with a Yak and Geelong blend, it is very warm and ideal to snuggle up under on the sofa on a cold winter evening.

The centre of the throw is garter stitch knitted from one corner, but there is no reason why it could not be changed and knitted with a lacy centre for the throw if preferred. Cat's Paw Lace or Diamonds would work well.

The throw is knitted from the centre out. It is also possible to knit it from the outside into the centre if wished. If this is your chosen approach then you will find it helpful to look at resources that explain the anatomy of the construction of traditional Hap shawls before you begin so that you can decide on the approach with which you feel happiest.

Before starting to knit, experiment with your chosen yarn, try different needle sizes to ensure that you knit a fabric that you are happy with, use this pattern as a template or make your own calculations based on the border pattern being an 18-stitch repeat. Make it as big or as small as you want. Whilst the colours that are used for this throw are included, there is no reason whatsoever why you should not choose whatever range of colours works for you.

As this throw is knitted from the inside out, it minimizes any sewing other than ends, and means that grafting together sections of the shawl is not required.

Once the centre has been completed, the throw is knitted in the round, with alternate rounds being purl in order to obtain an all over garter stitch pattern. This has the advantage of allowing you to knit and make it as big as you want, rather than establishing the size before you start and knitting from

Hap throw.

the outside in, although the latter is the traditional method employed by knitters in the Shetland Islands.

The throw is finished with a traditional peaked edging which is knitted on.

Instructions for Knitting

The centre of the throw is knitted first and starts in one corner. Cast on 1 st.

Row 1: yo, k into back of st.

Row 2: continue in this way, increasing one stitch with a yarn over on every row and knitting into the back of the last stitch of every row until there are 268 sts (or desired amount) on the needle. Now start the decrease as follows: yo, slip one, knit 2 together, pass slip stitch over, knit to end of the row, knit into back of the last stitch. Continue decreasing in this manner, one stitch on each row until 2 stitches remain, k 2 together.

Without breaking yarn with the remaining stitch from the centre as your first stitch, pick up 134 loops down each side of the throw centre, placing a marker for the corners after each 134th stitch.

Next round: knit these stitches through the back of the loop whilst at the same time increasing 14 sts evenly across each quarter of the throw. 148 stitches per side.

Continue knitting in the round as follows.

Set Up Rows

Next row k.

Next p.

Next round: (k2tog, yo) to last st before marker, k1 sm (148sts).

Next and all even-numbered rounds: purl.

Now start main chart pattern.

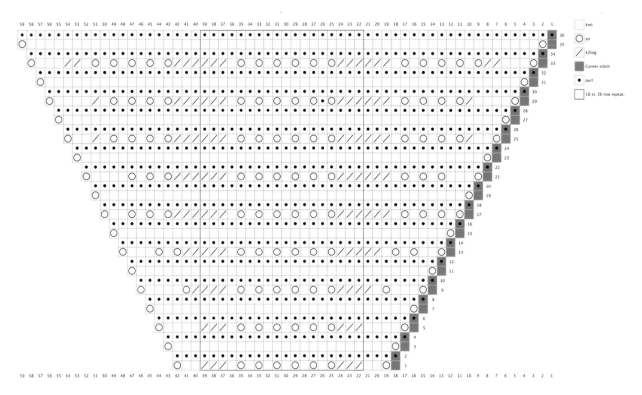

Main chart for Old Shell edging.

Hap Throw written instructions

Round 1: K1, yo, k2, k2tog × 3, (yo, k1) × 6, k2tog × 3, k2, yo. (25 sts)

Round 2 and all even-numbered rounds: Purl.

Round 3: K1, yo, k24, yo. (27 sts)

Round 5: K1, yo, k4, k2tog × 3, (yo, k1) × 6, k2tog × 3, k4, yo. (29 sts)

Round 7: K1, yo, k28, yo. (31 sts)

Round 9: K1, yo, k3, yo, k1, k2tog × 4, (yo, k1) × 6, k2tog × 4, yo, k4, yo. (33 sts)

Round 11: K1, yo, k32, yo. (35 sts)

Round 13: K1, yo, k2, (yo, k1) × 2, k2tog × 5, (yo, k1) × 6, k2tog × 5, yo, k1, yo, k3, yo. (37 sts)

Round 15: K1, yo, k36, yo. (39 sts)

Round 17: ((K1, yo) × 4, k1, k2tog × 6, yo, k1, yo) × 2, k1, yo, k2, yo. (41 sts)

Round 19: K1, yo, k40, yo. (43 sts)

Round 21: K1, yo, k3, (yo, k1) × 3, k2tog × 6, (yo, k1) × 6, k2tog × 6, (yo, k1) × 2, yo, k4, yo. (45 sts)

Round 23: K1, yo, k44, yo. (47 sts)

Round 25: K1, yo, k2, k2tog, ((yo, k1) × 4, k2tog × 6, (yo, k1) × 2) × 2, (yo, k1) × 2, k2tog, k2, yo. (49 sts)

Round 27: K1, yo, k48, yo. (51 sts)

Round 29: K1, yo, k4, k2tog, (yo, k1) × 4, k2tog × 6, yo, p1, (yo, k1) × 5, k2tog × 6, (yo, k1) × 4, k2tog, k4, yo. (53 sts)

Round 31: K1, yo, k52, yo. (55 sts)

Round 33: K1, yo, k3, k2tog × 2, ((yo, k1) × 5, k2tog × 6, yo, k1) × 2, (yo, k1) × 4, k2tog × 2, k3, yo. (57 sts)

Round 35: K1, yo, k56, yo. (59 sts)

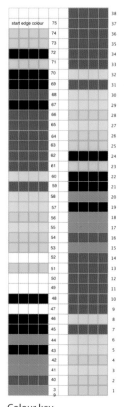

Colour key.

Once you have completed the edging to whatever depth you wish, you can add the knitted-on edging if you want, or alternatively leave the Old Shell as it is, it will create a very pleasing wavy edge once cast off.

If you wish to include the traditional peaked edging, then at the beginning of a pattern repeat and with the yarn colour that you wish to use for the edging, work a round of yo, k2tog, increasing the number of stitches evenly along each side of the throw to multiples of ten, keeping the yarn overs as established on either side of each corner stitch.

Next round. Purl. At the end of the round with WS facing and using the knitted on or lace cast on, cast on 17 sts. Purl these stitches back to the last 3 cast on sts, yo, k2tog, knit the last cast on stitch with the first stitch from the main knitting on LH needle. Turn and start edging chart knitting the last edging stitch together with the next stitch on the LH needle on every WS row. *See* instructions for knitting on an edging in Chapter 3 – Techniques.

For the chart and written instructions for the traditional peaked edging used in this pattern, turn to Chapter 4, where these will be found in the edgings section of the Stitchionary. You will find other potential options for edging the throw in this section should you wish to vary the photographed pattern.

When all the stitches have been cast off carefully, sew the two ends of the edging together using mattress st. Sew in loose ends. Wash and block to size.

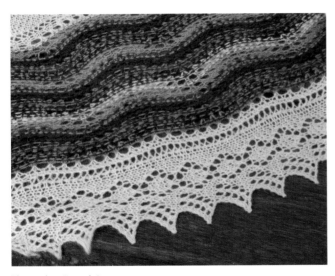

Throw showing edging.

Throw showing corner detail.

Crest of the Wave Cushion Cover

- This cushion is made from dk 50/50 linen silk blend.
- Three 1in ×1in buttons.
- The cover is for a standard 16in cushion pad.
- Gauge is 20 × 25 to 4in or 10cm.
- You will need 3.75 mm needles or size to obtain gauge.
- Button band is knitted on 2.75mm or equivalent, depending on needles used to obtain gauge.
- 2 dpns 2.75 or size used for button band to make the i-cord piping.

Instructions for Knitting

Front.

Using 3.75 mm needles cast on 65 sts in dark green.

Knit 4 rows in garter st.

Change to pale green.

Start chart and complete 8 full pattern repeats, changing colour as indicated on the chart.

Cast off all sts.

Crest of the Wave cushion cover.

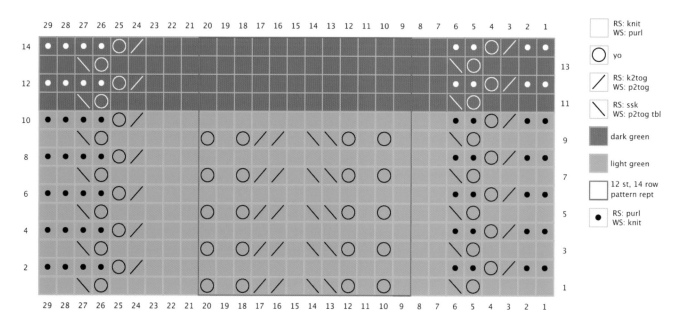

Chart for front of cushion showing colour changes.

Legend:

- RS: knit / WS: purl
- ○ yo
- / RS: k2tog / WS: p2tog
- \ RS: ssk / WS: p2tog tbl
- dark green
- light green
- 12 st, 14 row pattern rept
- • RS: purl / WS: knit

Crest of the Wave Cushion Cover Instructions

Row 1 (RS): K4, yo, ssk, k3, yo, k, yo, ssk × 2, k, k2tog × 2, yo, k, yo, k5, yo, ssk, k2 (29 sts).

Row 2 and all WS rows: K4, yo, p2tog, p17, k2, yo, p2tog, k2.

Row 3: Repeat row 1.

Row 5: Repeat row 1.

Row 7: Repeat row 1.

Row 9: Repeat row 1.

Row 10: K4, yo, p2tog, p17, k2, yo, p2tog, k2.

Change to dark green.

Row 11–14: K4, yo, ssk, k19, yo, ssk, k2.

Cushion Lower Back

With 3.75mm needles and pale green yarn cast on 82 sts.

The first 2 and last 2 sts of every row are knit.

Work in st for 10 rows.

Change to dark green yarn and knit rows 11–14

Change to pale green and repeat these 14 rows, making the colour changes as set until work measures 12in.

Knit 4 rows in pale green.

Cast off all stitches.

Upper Back

Using 2.75mm needles co 82 sts in dark green.

K 1 row.

Change to pale green and continue in garter stitch for 16 rows.

Button hole row. K13, make button hole.

Bring yarn to front, slip st pw. Place yarn at back and leave.

Slip next st from left hand needle, pass first sl st over.

Repeat from * 9 more times, 10 sts bound off.

Sl last bound off st to left needle, turn work.

Using a cable cast on, cast on 11 sts, turn work.

Sl first st with yarn at back from left needle and pass extra cast on st over.

One button hole made.

(Button hole size can be adjusted by casting off more or less sts depending upon button size.)

Complete row, making two further button holes spaced 13 stitches apart.

Knit 16 further rows.

Change to dark green.

K 2 rows.

Change to 3.75 mm and to pale green yarn.

Continue in st st until work measures 8in.

Cast off all sts.

To make up, wet block pieces to measurements. Sew in ends. Join side seams using back st matching stripes from front and back. Attach buttons.

To make I-cord, using dpns size 2.75mm, cast on 7 st.

Knit to end of row, pull st on left hand needle back up the needle, pull yarn across back of work and knit. Continue in this manner until I-cord will fit around the seam line of the cushion, easing it to fit neatly round the corners. Cast off, stitch in place and join ends neatly so they do not show.

Completed cushion back view.

Bibliography

Yarn suppliers

Abbey, Barbara, *Barbara Abbey's Knitting Lace*
(Schoolhouse Press.)

Bush, Nancy, *Knitted Lace of Estonia. Techniques, Patterns and Traditions* (Interweave Press llc)

Compton, Rae, *The Complete Book of Traditional Knitting* (Batsford)

Don, Sarah, *The Art of Shetland Lace* (Mills and Boon)

Khmeleva, Galina, & Noble, Carol R., *Gossamer Webs. The History and Techniques of Orenburg Lace Shawls* (Interweave Press llc)

Lovick, Elizabeth, *The Magic of Shetland Lace Knitting* (Search Press)

Lovick, Elizabeth, *The Same, but Different: Shetland Lace in a European Context* (kbth Lace Virtual Conference, March 2006)

Miller, Sharon, *Heirloom Knitting. A Shetland Lace Knitter's Pattern and Workbook* (The Shetland Times Ltd.)

Mrs Gaugin, *The Lady's Assistant for Executing Useful and Fancy Designs in Knitting, Netting and Crochet Work* (1840)

Norbury, James, *Traditional Knitting Patterns* (Dover Publications Inc.)

Reimann, Leili, *Pitsilised Koekirjad* (Valgus 1986)

Reimann, Siiri, & Edasi, Aime, *The Haapsalu Shawl. A Knitted Lace Tradition from Estonia* (Saara Publishing House)

Rutt, Richard, *A History of Hand Knitting* (Batsford)

Stanley, Montse, *Knitter's Hand Book* (Reader's Digest)

Thomas, Mary, *Mary Thomas's Book of Knitting Patterns* (Dover Publications, Inc.)

Walker, Barbara G., *A Second Treasury of Knitting Patterns* (Schoolhouse Press)

Walker, Barbara G., *A Treasury of Knitting Patterns* (Schoolhouse Press)

Weldon's Practical Needlework, circa 1895

All samples in the Stitchionary were knitted with one ply Cobweb lace weight from Jamieson and Smith, Lerwick, Shetland
www.shetlandwoolbrokers.co.uk.

ColourMart kindly supported the acquisition of yarns for this book and were the source of the yarns used for the Hap throw, the lacy socks, the Fir Cone scarf and the lace wedding wraps as well as the majority of the yarn sample motifs. They can be found at http://www.colourmart.com/.

Jamiesons of Shetland
http://www.jamiesonsofshetland.co.uk/.

Gongcrafts. Suppliers of hand carded and spun naturally dyed yarn from the Far North of Scotland
http://www.facebook.com/Gongcrafts.

Acknowledgements

I would particularly like to thank the Lerwick Textile Museum and the Unst Heritage Centre for providing access to their collections; the Knitting and Crochet Guild for providing photographs from their collection; Angharad Thomas, photographer of the Orenburg lace shawl; RogueKnit on Ravelry for allowing me to use her picture of 'Four Seasons: The Winter', an Orenburg shawl designed by Russian Lily, also on Ravelry; Audrey Lincoln and Ann Way for assisting with knitting; Natalie Bullock for her help as both model and photographer; Sophie Thomson, model; Zoe and Tom Green for the use of the wedding photo with the Harebell Lace wrap; Richard Skins wedding photographer; Rita Taylor for all her support and advice; Loraine McClean for her positivity, encouragement and for getting me involved with this project in the first place! And most especially Sophie Thomson and Thea Sullivan for all their support and encouragement.

Index